Caroline Wane

3/02

"I know of no woman of our time who has made a richer and more significant contribution, in a truly contemporary way, to man's understanding of himself. Her essays, particularly those on old age, are among the finest and the most rounded things she has ever done."

—Sir Laurens van der Post

"I have been so much impressed by the essays on *The Odyssey* and *The Tempest* . . . a depth is revealed in them which I would never have expected."

—Father Bede Griffiths

"In these five essays, Helen Luke writes about classic texts with an easy grace that belies the depth and precision of her thoughts on the transformative mysteries of old age and suffering. We feel her much as she describes Nausicaa: 'a truly human woman. . . . Intelligent, courageous . . . not at all naïve, she has already the dignity of the woman who can love without demand to possess.'"

—Charles H. Taylor

"A jewel, glittering with new and astonishing insights about the psychological tasks of later life."

—Allan B. Chinen

THEO., spty

ALSO BY HELEN M. LUKE

SUCH STUFF AS DREAMS ARE MADE ON:
The Autobiography and Journals of Helen M. Luke

KALEIDOSCOPE:
The Way of Woman and Other Essays

DARK WOOD TO WHITE ROSE:
Journey and Transformation in Dante's *Divine Comedy*

THE WAY OF WOMAN:
Awakening the Perennial Feminine

OLD AGE

Journey into Simplicity

HELEN M. LUKE

Foreword by Thomas Moore

Introduction by Barbara A. Mowat

Bell Tower · New York

A PARABOLA BOOK

A complete list of permissions appears on page 135.

"The Odyssey," "The Tempest," and "Little Gidding" were originally published in 1985 as a pamphlet by Apple Farm Community, Three Rivers, Michigan. "King Lear" was originally published in 1982 in *The Inner Story*, a Crossroads book, copyright Helen M. Luke. "Suffering" originally appeared in *Parabola*, VIII:l, January 1983.

Published by Bell Tower, New York, New York.
Member of the Crown Publishing Group.

Random House, Inc. New York, Toronto, London, Sydney, Auckland
www.randomhouse.com

Bell Tower and colophon are registered trademarks of Random House, Inc.

Originally published, in slightly different form, by Parabola in 1987.

Printed in the United States of America

Design by Susan Maksuta

Library of Congress Cataloging-in-Publication Data

Luke, Helen M., 1904–1995.
    Old age / Helen M. Luke ; foreword by Thomas Moore.— 1st ed.
    Includes bibliographical references.
        1. English literature—History and criticism. 2. Old age in literature. 3. Eliot, T. S. (Thomas Stearns), 1888–1965. *Four quartets*. 4. Shakespeare, William, 1564–1616. *King Lear*. 5. Shakespeare, William, 1564–1616. *Tempest*. 6. Odysseus (Greek mythology) in literature. 7. Homer. *Odyssey*. I. Title.
    PR409.O45 L8 2001
    809'.93354—dc21   00-057930

ISBN 0-609-80590-8

10 9 8 7 6 5 4 3 2 1

First Bell Tower Edition

CONTENTS

Quick now, here, now, always—
A condition of complete simplicity
(Costing not less than everything)

T. S. Eliot
"Little Gidding"

FOREWORD

As I write these words I am two months away from my six-tieth birthday. As the decades pile up, new thoughts arrive spontaneously. I think about the age people are as they die around me. Bodily pains and failures have more of the weight of mortality about them, and I wonder what form death will take. I'm aware that my daughter is only eight years old and will probably live most of her life without me. My wife is con-siderably younger than I, and I think about her going on after me. Of course, God's plan is always full of surprises, but these fantasies are significant in themselves, no matter what hap-pens. They are the soul expressing itself on this day, not just literally about the future but about its situation at the moment.

What I treasure about Helen Luke's remarkable book about old age is that she avoids getting caught up in all the usual wor-ries and sentimentalities. She sees age as a mystery and quite rightly hangs all her thoughts about it on images from litera-ture. And not just literature, but some of the most profound of all imaginative writings, which just happen to be personal favorites of mine.

Her models of aging are eccentrics and fools—holy fools, of course: Odysseus, Lear, and Prospero. I take it that the best way to move into old age is to allow the fool to come forward, to become more and not less an individual following mad attractions. But to perceive and allow the fool, it's necessary to see through the obvious and the literal and grasp the mysterious that plays out in the less ambitious, less focused control of life. The beauty of this book is that it isn't so much about aging as about the soul's process, its ongoing alchemy, responding to changes in the body, in life, and in one's sense of self.

For me the core of this book about the enchantment of age is the theme of Prospero giving up his magic book and his guiding angel and his staff. It looks as though Helen Luke had given up her own magic book when she wrote this one. It is free of instruction, ambition, and the pose of wisdom. I will never forget two statements from other authors she cites: Laurens van der Post—"total surrender to the truth of himself"—and Charles Williams—"I'll break all imposition of views." She is talking about the art of release, the surrender of self, and the paradoxical discovery of what has always been present but never fully embraced.

She writes about forgiveness and prayer, two items we think we know something about, until they become translucent in old age and play central roles in the embrace of one's life and one's world. And the place of mercy in this process. She sees the *merc-* of mercy in the words "merchant" and "commercially," and points out the importance of exchange and courtesy in old age. But she doesn't mention the *merc-* in *Mercury,* yet Mercury, the imagination at its most free and playful, runs through her entire book as she makes one giant play on aging. The capacity to see through, to see deeply enough, to see what is not obviously present—these are the gifts of this wonderful little Mercurial book.

I confess I might have expected Helen Luke to be more Jungian here, more explanatory, more psychologically clever. She isn't any of these things. Every sentence flows from many hours of reflection and an openness to experience. She does what a good artist does: she dreams the dream onward, not leaving the realm of mystery for the crisper air of understanding. She offers a gentle push toward an imagination of age, but she doesn't offer a program or a theory. As I say, she practices what she preaches, giving up her own angels and, it appears, her precious ideas.

The reader is invited to do likewise, and you don't have to wait for old age to do it. As Helen Luke intimates, aging is a matter of imagination. You may be disappointed not to find another plan for aging gracefully. If so, give up the expectation. Give up the need for a theory. Break the staff of your need. Drown the book that has become your life manual and proceed to forgiveness and mercy. Read this book and pray.

Thomas Moore

INTRODUCTION

IN THE ESSAYS that make up this reflection on old age, Helen M. Luke, who has written so perceptively about myth and symbol in life and in art, presents us with perhaps her greatest gift yet: her very potent insights into a phase of life that until now has not been fully incorporated into our understanding of the inner journey. Many men and women today are aware of the tasks of the "second half of life," aware that (as Helen Luke expresses it) "having eaten the apple and chosen to know good and evil," we have left "the infantile Paradise" to "go individually on the long journey in the dimension of time in which each [learns] through the bitter conflicts of the opposites to discriminate every smallest thing or image as unique and separate." We have glimpsed as our goal that "'objective cognition' which Jung called the central secret" have begun to distinguish "the ego from the Self which is ours and not ours." But that is not the end of the journey. A further, crucial step remains—and it is that step, that transition into the last phase

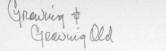
Growing & Growing Old

of our journey toward death, that Helen Luke addresses in this book, *Old Age*.

Drawing on the masterworks of Homer, Dante, Shakespeare, and T. S. Eliot; reading those works with an understanding formed through years of absorbing and reflecting upon the insights of Carl Jung; and speaking as a wonderfully conscious individual making the transition herself into old age, Helen Luke teaches us that a point comes in our lives at which we *choose* how we go into our last years, how we approach our death. The choice, as she describes it, may be painful, requiring (should we choose to continue to *grow* old, instead of merely sinking into the aging process) that we let go of much that has been central even to our inner lives. The choice, she says at one point, is "whether [we] will let go of everything else so that a new man who is the creation of Mercy will be born, or whether [we] will hold on to the old man, to rejection of that emptiness which is the fullness of Mercy."

As is so often the case in Helen Luke's writings, the great images that she finds for us are in familiar literary texts, though the images need her special perceptiveness to reveal their meanings to us. Others, for example, may have noticed that, buried within the text of Homer's *Odyssey,* is a description of Odysseus' final journey—a sacrificial journey, alone, away from the sea—a journey very different from that given to Odysseus by Dante in *The Inferno*. Helen Luke has seen that the Homeric and the Dantesque journeys are, in fact, images of the paths that each of us may choose between as we, like Odysseus, approach old age—the one path tempting us toward repetition

14

of our life's triumphs, tempting us toward wreckage and the inferno, the other coaxing us toward the true journey of the soul that has lived long and well, and that must turn away from mere continuation of accustomed efforts to new, significant, perhaps painful, soul-journeys to plant oars in desert lands and to offer in sacrifice our past strengths and triumphs.

The image of Odysseus' two possible journeys, of Lear "embracing his prison," of Prospero choosing to forgive, choosing to release Ariel, seeking Mercy, finding sustenance in the needed "other"—these lead Helen Luke (and lead us through her) into startling insights about what our last years can hold for us. Those years (whenever they come for us: for William Shakespeare, for Charles Williams, for Thomas Merton, they came early) may well be very difficult—may be, as Helen Luke notes, especially difficult for those "whose lives have been spent in the service of a creative spirit." Every man and woman, she writes, "must, like Prospero, come at last to the point of recognizing that this 'spirit' . . . will not remain forever at the beck and call of his ego, giving him a sense of meaning and achievement in his life to the end." When this moment comes, "all too often it may itself be refused, unrecognized. Ariel is held on to—the 'winged life' is destroyed and the possibility of growth into death recedes. There may follow a desperate effort to hold on to youth and the past, to arrest the flow of the river of life as it approaches the ocean of eternity; or else the apathy of meaninglessness that Prospero feared may invade the psyche. So old age becomes decay, not in the natural sense of the cycle of life and death but in the negative and horrible sense of disintegration and despair."

For those who recognize the moment, who choose to let go, to embrace "the gifts reserved for age": loss of energy and of enchantment, helpless rage at the folly of mankind, the suffering hidden in our memories—old age becomes freedom, becomes the dance "into which we may enter if we have passed through . . . the purging flame of integration of these strange gifts." The wonder of the dance, of the Mercy, of the laughter that lie on the other side of the letting go—these are what stay with us as we read and reread Helen Luke's reflections on the rites of passage that precede our final passage into death. What we remember is that

the "pattern of the glory" (as Charles Williams calls it) is not, as we have perhaps imagined, an apex of achievement, even in the inner world of the soul and the spirit. Rather is it known in the agonies and dangers of a gradual letting go, through which alone the emptiness comes, into which the glory may enter.

Barbara A. Mowat
Folger Shakespeare Library

OLD AGE

THE ODYSSEY

THERE ARE TWO epilogues to *The Odyssey*. One was written by Homer and the other many centuries later by Dante. They are alternative endings to the life of Odysseus, the hero, and the fact that the second was imagined so long after the original poem in no way invalidates it. All great stories are continued by those who respond to them, as long as their truth endures; and myths that cease to grow through the centuries will die. Dante had not even read *The Odyssey* (it is known that he did not read Greek), but he had heard the story. Since he was a poet as great as Homer, the image of his meeting with Ulysses in *The Inferno* is still as alive today as Homer's original story. To Dante's alternative and its meaning we shall return later.

Homer's epilogue, it seems, is overlooked by most readers, probably because it is not actually narrated at the end of the poem. It is prophesied, however, about halfway through the book, told by Teiresias, the blind seer, who, when he meets Odysseus at the border of Hades, describes the whole course of the journey that lies ahead for him. After telling of his possible homecoming and the end of his conflicts, Teiresias adds a last prophecy: there still remains for the hero another journey in his old age. He must set out once again from his home, but this time it will not be a sea journey, although he must carry with him a well-cut oar. Turning inland he must travel on until he reaches a country where the people have never seen the sea, have never tasted salt, and know nothing about ships; he will recognize the right place when he meets a stranger, who, seeing the oar, will ask him about the "winnowing fan" he is carrying on his shoulder.

At this spot he is to halt and plant his oar firmly in the earth; then he must make a sacrifice to Poseidon—"a ram, a bull, and a breeding boar"[1]—and when he returns home he must make "ceremonial offering" to all of the immortal gods in heaven—to each of them in order.

This done, Odysseus will settle down amongst his powerful and prosperous people, says Teiresias, until he is weary with rich old age, and then he ends: "Death will come to you out of the sea, Death in his gentlest guise . . . This is the truth that I have told you."[2]

Everything foretold by Teiresias except this epilogue is described by Homer in great detail as it happens. That he had not forgotten it and did not minimize its importance is clear when Odysseus, on his first night of reunion with Penelope, telling her his story, warns her of this journey and of the separation to be endured. So it is surprising that the poem ends with the intervention of Zeus that brought peace to the warring factions in Ithaca and a conclusion to Odysseus' fighting days, and no more is told of this strange last journey.

Nevertheless the mysterious epilogue of Teiresias' vision, if it has touched the imagination of the reader, may rise again in our memory, as we read of this peace imposed by all-powerful Zeus—imposed even upon his daughter, Athene, who was still inciting Odysseus with considerable vigor to revengeful war upon his fellow citizens.

It is possible that the story of the last quiet journey of the storm-tossed, all-conquering hero was not told in the final version of *The Odyssey* that has come down to us because it seemed an anticlimax, possibly boring to listeners who would not understand it. But it is there, embedded forever in the words of the wise old man who spoke to Odysseus at a great turning point in his life's journey, when he had still so much to learn about himself and the meaning of life. It comes to life again as of vital importance when Odysseus warns Penelope of still more suffering to come. At the time of his meeting with Teiresias beside the blood from his sacrifice on the border of Hades, he was still identified with the hero image of himself, acquired in his ten years as a brave warrior and the shrewdest tactician of the age, revered by all his fellows in the war against Troy. Indeed it was his arrogance in this role after leaving Troy that brought upon him the implacable enmity of Poseidon, Earth-shaker and God of the Sea.

Not only had Odysseus insisted on exploring the island of the Cyclops against the advice of his companions but, when captured by Polyphemos, the Cyclops, son of Poseidon, he had

escaped after putting out the single eye of the giant, and had
then proceeded to shout insults from his boat at his blinded
enemy. His crew begged him to desist since he invited their
death, goading Polyphemos into hurling great rocks which
almost destroyed them; but he went on boasting. "I would not
heed them in my glorifying spirit."[3] He taunted Polyphemos,
calling his blindness shameful and naming himself "a great
sacker of cities." Polyphemos' fury was thus kindled, and he
cried to his father for revenge. Poseidon heard him; and this
was the cause of Odysseus' ten additional years of disastrous
wanderings and loss of all his companions. His ten years of
masculine achievement in the Trojan war had degenerated
into an aggressive inflation. He could not let go of his identification with the hero. Therefore during the next ten years most
of his experiences involved confrontations with various aspects
of the feminine unconscious, personified by secondary goddesses who cast their varying spells on him and his men: Circe,
who turns men into swine; the Sirens, luring men to destruction; Scylla with her twelve devouring mouths; Calypso, who
kept him for years a prisoner on her island, offering him
immortality in exchange for his love, until at last the great goddess Athene pleaded with Zeus, and he was released.

It is perhaps the greatest story in Western literature of a
man's journey in search of his feminine soul and of the dangers
he must face from the rejected feeling values of the unconscious. Even after his release from Calypso it is not until he has
lost his raft and endured nine days of buffeting by storm and
wave that he is finally cast up naked and alone on the shore of
the land of the Phaiakians. Here he is rescued and befriended

at last by a truly human woman, the princess Nausicaa, who is assuredly one of the most enchanting young women in the stories of the world. Intelligent, courageous, wholly natural, and spontaneous, but not at all naive, she has already the dignity of the woman who can love without demand to possess. She has a human simplicity which is total delight after the spells and magical attractions of Circe and Calypso.

The greatness of Homer's storytelling strikes deep into the heart in the lovely passage telling of their meeting. Every detail is described with such vivid simplicity that one is transported straight into that time and place. It is not a matter of only hearing about these people and things; we live in them. It begins with the dream, sent by Athene, to Nausicaa, and the lovely description of her as she gathers the washing of the family and goes with her young maids in the mule cart to the clear pools near the beach. Then we watch her in her grace and beauty, as she plays after work, tossing a ball with her companions, and suddenly the naked Odysseus emerges from the bushes, bloated and salt-encrusted from his long hours in the sea. The maids all run away but Nausicaa meets this frightening sight with her natural compassion, with courtesy and good sense, and we know for a moment the meaning of innocence.

In his hero's first meeting with a human woman after all those years, Homer was surely hinting at the qualities which we sense in Penelope herself at the end—qualities matured by her long suffering. It was Odysseus' ultimate faithfulness to Penelope, his human wife—and his refusal of the immortality offered by Calypso—his longing to return to his human beloved, that had brought him to this meeting with Nausicaa, without whose shrewd feminine wisdom and feeling he might have been thrust back to sea by the islanders. (It was she who told him to be sure to appeal to her mother the queen *first*, before approaching her father!)

I like to think that Penelope in her youth had this same quality of lighthearted yet shrewd innocence, and that, after her long years of suffering and almost, but never quite, hopeless waiting, the laughter and innocence of maturity would be in her a source of strength to all whose lives she touched when, after Odysseus' last unrecorded journey, she would share with him the wisdom of the richly old. Robert Fitzgerald has pointed out in the Postscript to his translation that a careful reading of her words and actions, after she sees and meets with Odysseus on his return disguised as a beggar, reveals her as a strategist every bit as intelligent as her husband, and even lets us glimpse her long hidden gift of laughter.

After hearing that I was writing on old age in reference to *The Odyssey* and *The Tempest*, someone asked me a question about old age in a woman. It had not in fact occurred to me that the kind of experience I imagined would differ essentially in the two sexes, though of course its outer manifestations are unique for every single individual, man or woman, as are also the symbolic images through which the transformations come to each. The point at issue is the "motive in the ground of our beseeching"[4]—the final letting go of all profit motives, on all the levels of our being—the end of all demand for results. In the feminine psyche, the hidden power and profit motives are usually concerned with the shadow side of relationships, the subtle desire to possess and manipulate those close to us, or else to be supported, even possessed, by the love of others for the sake of protection from danger, loneliness, and responsibility. The unconscious in a man has similar problems of jealousy and possessiveness, but in the main his danger lies, as it did for both Prospero and for Odysseus, in the exercise of power in the outer world, whether as hero or magician. In our day, as a woman works and excels more and more in the spheres hitherto reserved for men, her power motives have become more visible in the operations of her animus, the personification of the masculine powers in her unconscious; therefore she must consciously watch the odyssey of her masculine creativity, and when she comes to the choice between the two possible "last journeys" of the kind offered to Odysseus it is for her, perhaps, an even greater moment of danger. For if she chooses another voyage of achievement, still longing to be herself a hero or despising the inner feminine way of Penelope, the waiting, the weaving of the threads of life into the whole cloth of a shroud—this time a joyful womb of death from which the new man, the new woman, may be born—then her animus will cease to serve her creative spirit and will drag her down to another death. This in no way implies a necessity to give up so-called masculine work in the world.

It is essentially an inner journey for man and woman alike: the forests, the jungles, the deserts, the times of weariness and despair. The wisdom and the grace which have come to us through the active years of our lives will be there through it all, trusted still, but often no longer personally felt, and casting a darker shadow when we cling to them for support and guidance. We imagine Odysseus plodding on day by day, step by step, and perhaps some will remember Frodo in *The Lord of the Rings* as the weight of the Ring of Power grew heavier on that last lap of his journey to Mt. Doom where he must destroy it. So for Odysseus, too, the oar he carried must have grown a heavier burden, as the realization grew in his thought that the moment when he could be relieved of its weight would also be the moment of the final letting go of that which had held for him the meaning of his life. The horizon for such travellers shrinks and shrinks until they are stripped of all but the present moment—then indeed it may expand into eternity.

Odysseus, after his victory over the suitors, goes to his father Laertes in his country retreat and makes himself known. While he is there the fathers of some of the suitors raise a band of armed citizens to revenge them. Athene is, as usual, around, and in spite of Zeus's expressed desire for peace, when the citizens attack Odysseus and he repulses them, she leaps ahead urging Odysseus to destroy them. But her father Zeus—usually so indulgent to her desires—sends a thunderbolt to stop her, and peace is finally established in Ithaca with general goodwill. Here the poem ends. No epilogue follows—no account of the journey which Teiresias foretold and of which Odysseus had warned Penelope.

Each of us is free to imagine the events of Odysseus' last journey. Here is my own version.

EPILOGUE

THE PLANTING OF THE OAR

Odysseus now set about establishing the peace and goodwill ordained by Zeus, enjoying the longed-for reunion with Penelope, watching the young radiant manhood of his son and the serene old age of his father. But gradually as the years passed the restlessness came upon him and increased. After his father's death he felt freer and began to dream of discovering new lands, of sailing again to the west, even past the pillars of Hercules to the unknown southern seas. (This is the epilogue that Dante imagined as the chosen death of Ulysses.) Athene had befriended him before; might she not do so again? He had defeated the final attacks of his enemy Poseidon and this once offended god would surely have forgotten by now the injury to his son Polyphemos. Slowly and unconsciously the arrogance that had caused his long sufferings returned—working, as it always does, through the best of his human qualities—through his longing to know and to see all the wonders of creation and to understand things as yet hidden from most men. Beloved of his subjects and with his son grown to maturity to hold the country safe, he began to think he could easily take one more voyage over the wine-dark sea in a swift, well-built ship with some of his friends and a trusty crew. Penelope would understand and be exposed to no danger now.

One day he sat alone on a high cliff gazing out to sea, plans teeming in his head. He would delay no longer. The sun was hot. He found a tree and lay down in the shade to rest, his decision made; and soon he slept and there came to him a dream.

There was in the dream no warrior goddess to encourage him, but rather a memory. Once more he stood, as long ago, on the borders of the darkness of Hades; once more he slaughtered a black ewe and poured out the blood that the shades might speak to him; and once more he heard the voice of Teiresias the blind seer.

"Odysseus," the old man said, "you sleep indeed—and I do not mean your body but that shrewd mind that has been your great gift from the gods. Often you have misused it and brought great suffering on yourself and others, but you stand on the threshold of old age and the exploits you plan come from your inner blindness and not from the wisdom that is truly yours. I am that voice of wisdom in you, whose eyes are closed to that outer world but are clear and see far and near into the meanings of life.

"A great poet, blind as I am, will tell the story of your journeyings from Troy through the long years until your return to Ithaca. He is a storyteller who will make you immortal, a hero beyond time. But there shall come another poet as great and likewise unsurpassed in the telling of stories. This poet will tell that he, still living, and led by another great one, met you in the deep pit of hell, enclosed forever in a burning flame among the 'deceivers.' He knew some of your story, and asked to speak with you. This poet will imagine in unforgettable lines your final sailing beyond the pillars of the Western world in high hope and with the ever-increasing ambition of your exploring mind towards the southern pole for month after month, five moons in all, until you see ahead of you on the horizon a great mountain rising out of the sea towards heaven. With cries of eagerness you urge your crew towards it, but there comes a huge wave rolling from the mountain, becoming a whirlpool as it sucks your ship, yourself and all your companions down into the depths to join the shades below. The mountain is for this poet of the future the image of the climb that brings all men who approach it, if they are girdled with humility, to the vision of God in his totality. To this mountain and the glory beyond, this poet would come, knowing perhaps that the fate he imagined had befallen you could also have been his, had his yearning for knowledge possessed him to his undoing.[5]

"I shall say no more except that I already told you many years ago of the alternative journey you are now called to take—a journey which does indeed lie on the slopes of that mountain but holds no fame or glory for you; only loneliness and sadness. The choice is yours. Will you deceive yourself as Dante's Ulysses did in a sin far worse than the deceit of the Trojan horse?"

The voice ceased, the vision faded, and Odysseus woke.

He sat on as the sun sank in the red and golden sky, and he indeed remembered. He was appalled that the words of Teiresias all those years ago had been so completely blotted out from his conscious mind; and he remembered many other things too, every one of his adventures in turn with their moments of courage, skill, faithfulness, pride, cunning, deceit, and folly. Most vividly of all came the memory of that foolish arrogance which had been the beginning of the evils brought upon him by the great god of the sea. He remembered the adolescent stubbornness that had made him close his ears to the pleadings of his crew and recognized with shame that his present intention to show that, even in old age, he could equal the dangerous exploits of youth came from the very same root of pride and disregard of all the values of relatedness. Care for his wife's feelings, for the needs of his people and the lives of his crew—all these had been blotted out again. He saw once more the horror of the closed cave where the giant Cyclops devoured his men two by two, and the thought of his ingenuity in saving some of them and himself by trickery and the blinding of Polyphemos no longer brought the old satisfaction. For he also remembered other things he had never before allowed himself to recognize. Polyphemos' life was, until he came, the life of a simple shepherd tending his flocks and he, Odysseus, had thought only to rob him. He had not seen the giant eat or drink anything but milk, whey, and cheese before the invasion of the men whom he must have greatly feared as an unknown threat; and Polyphemos had cared for his sheep and lambs in a way which, in one so crude and ignorant, was gentle and thoughtful of their every need. For the first time Odysseus allowed himself to hear the voice of the Cyclops after his blinding, speaking to the leading ram of his flock, who was leaving the cave weighed down by Odysseus himself clinging to the wool under his belly.

Sweet cousin ram, why lag behind the rest
in the night cave? You never linger so,

but graze before them all, and go afar
to crop sweet grass, and take your stately way
leading along the streams, until at evening
you run to be the first one in the fold.
Why, now, so far behind? Can you be grieving
over your master's eye?[26]

With shame he realized, as he heard it in memory, the feeling in Polyphemos' crude breast for his animals and how he must have mourned their loss—not out of greed but out of love. And a strange new compassion awoke in his heart for one he had always thought of as nothing but a cannibal and a brute. Then he saw himself sailing away, hurling insults back, glorying in his prowess; and he knew he had nearly paid with the loss of the whole crew; indeed he did so pay with the lives of all those others in the years that followed.

After the deadening years of the siege of Troy, and the victory brought about by Odysseus' own great cunning with the deception of the Trojan horse, it was perhaps no great wonder that he had been puffed up with his own cleverness to such an extent that he had fallen into that arrogant folly so many years ago. He had paid through long years of bitter experiences, but he knew there could be no final forgiveness or peace for him if he fell again into that fever to discover the unknown at any cost, to be the unconquered one, dragging down yet again his friends, his wife, his crew into sorrow, despair, or death.

He rose to his feet in the twilight as the sun sank into the western sea. His choice was made. He knew that there was an old legend in the island, which no one took seriously, that somewhere in the interior in valleys among the mountains there were people who never came down to the shore, who indeed had no idea the sea existed. None of the seafaring islanders were interested in exploring the interior anyway and no one had ever tried to penetrate far. He had been told by the blind seer that he must take a well-cut oar and seek out these people. He did not understand—not yet—but he would obey. One thing was clear—this journey would bring no glory. Most men would deem it a foolish waste of time and think of him perhaps as already somewhat senile. Only Penelope would understand and rejoice. He was certain that she had not forgotten his telling her of Teiresias' prophecy on that night of their reunion, and he suddenly realized that she had spoken recently, once or twice, words which could have reminded him of this unfulfilled task, had he not been blinded by the glittering images of his longing to possess knowledge no other man had found, beyond the boundaries of the world. Never would she try to push him in his choices; but she knew, in her wisdom, of his danger and his need. And now his sense of sterile darkness in the final sacrifice of his heroic image of himself was taken up or down, as it were, into that quiet wisdom—wisdom that had always saved him in these moments of his extreme danger. The darkness would return and he had no illusions about the journey before him. It sounded easy in those few words of Teiresias, but he could not guess its length or the hardships of the way. He knew only that he must go, and go soon, and alone.

So he went quickly home and straight to Penelope's room. She looked at him with a question in her eyes and he knew she had waited once more in silence and fear for his choice. Now one look was enough—there was a surge of the joy that has passed beyond desire for both of them. They held each other and Odysseus said quietly, "Forgive me, Penelope, for what I have done to you of late. I will take my finest oar and go forth again, but this time, even if I should die, nothing can threaten the unity between us any more."

Odysseus set out alone. There were no maps to follow once he came to the last known village on the slopes of the hills. He must simply walk on into the unknown, following the tracks of animals in the forests, crossing the deserts on weary feet, climbing beside streams to their source. Beside him a small sturdy donkey carried his stores of food and the minimum of equipment for the way.

Odysseus struggled up a bare hillside track until he came at last to a crossroad where four tracks met and where he found a stranger watching him approach. Now he heard the words for which he had longed but which by now he had almost forgotten, sounding at last like a song of liberation in his heart: "What winnowing fan is that upon your shoulder?" With enormous relief he set down his burden, holding it as it rested on its handle, blade upwards; and, straightening his shoulders, he looked at the stranger and for the first time wondered whatever was the meaning of this question of which Teiresias had warned him. It cannot be, he thought, simply the ignorance of a man who never saw the sea.

The stranger was dressed like a peasant in a rough tunic and held a staff in his hand, but his face was sensitive and intelligence shone in his eyes, and humor showed in the generous mouth. "Why do you speak of a winnowing fan," said Odysseus, "when you must know very well that this is a beautiful oar with which I cleave the great waters of the wine-dark seas around us?" And as he spoke his eyes took on the faraway look of the sailor scanning wide horizons.

The stranger smiled and answered, "You are right, I am not ignorant of the oar—though you see below you here a village, or rather an encampment, where no man will recognize it. But nevertheless I was not pretending by using the words 'winnowing fan.' For I recognize you, Lord Odysseus, and I know your story—and it may be that you will come to recognize me, for you have glimpsed me now and then on your journeying. I ask you now only to think of the meaning of that image." Odysseus looked keenly at the other. "Why, the winnowing fan is something that creates a wind whereby the chaff is separated from the grain at the time of harvest. What has that to do with an oar?"

"Remember only what the oar has meant to you through the many years of your life, Odysseus. You have been brought, by the seer who is blind to outer shapes but who sees the shape of things within and their meaning in each man's life, to make this last journey precisely in order that you may finally recognize your own oar as a true winnowing fan. Do you not know that your travels, your achievements and failures, the gains and losses to which your winged ship carried you were all slowly forging for you a 'winnowing fan'? Now that the harvest is gathered and you stand in the autumn of your life, your oar is no longer a driving force carrying you over the oceans of your inner and outer worlds, but a spirit of discriminating wisdom, separating moment by moment the wheat of life from the chaff, so that you may know in both wheat and chaff their meaning and their value in the pattern of the universe. This final journey seemed pointless—indeed merely a kind of 'chaff' blowing in the wind, but you chose it nonetheless because at last you trusted the blind seer hidden in your heart, as Penelope has trusted him for so long."

There was a silence, and then Odysseus spoke, and his eyes were smiling. "Yes," he said, "I truly begin to look now through the blind eyes of the seer. But that being so, tell me, stranger, why I should plant this well-cut oar here and leave it where no one will know its uses or its meaning? Why should I not take it home—not for my own use any more, but maybe for my son's?"

"To leave it is essential, Odysseus. If you were to put it in your son's hands you would watch his sea journey through life, transferring to him your yearning for great deeds; you would never let go of the goals of youth. Moreover you might thus prevent your own son from carving his own oar from the wood, finding his own way. To leave it here is like a gift of your lifetime's effort to people who live here in such simplicity. They will see it and begin to ask questions—and travellers, I for one, will tell them about the great waters beyond their present horizons—of the wonders and dangers of the deep, of the beauty of swift ships, and of the tang of salt to be found there—salt which will always mean for future men and women the latent wisdom and humor and savor of the spirit. They will not understand these tales, but their bolder spirits will grow restless and curious, and they will leave home to seek for answers. Torn from their simple natural roots, they will suffer greatly as all men and women must ultimately suffer. A future legend will tell of this in an image of the first woman giving to the first man the apple of the knowledge of good and evil, and of their expulsion from the paradise of their unconscious unity with nature to begin the long journey over land and sea, through darkness and danger, through light and happiness, through doubt and faith, conflict and coherence, to the Return. It is a return to the same simplicity and oneness with nature and spirit that these people here have, but they live without understanding, as do beast and flower. In the Return, however, the oneness is known, experienced, through the awakening of the mind of God in each man and woman. That future now becomes possible for you, my friend. Come, I will help you dig a hole. You have a dagger, do you not? There is soft earth here in the center of this crossroad."

They set to work with hands and knife and, as the hole deepened, the stranger said, almost chanting as minstrels do, "I see your oar standing stark and meaningless in this place, but as the years go by and questions grow and multiply I see roots growing down into the earth and green shoots bearing leaves begin to spring out from the blade; and in the future, when the blind poet Homer has come here with the tale of your life, Odysseus, the blossoms and the fruit will break from the tree of your oar year after year, through aeons of time."

In silence they deepened the hole, set the oar in it, filled it again with earth, and finally collected stones to build a small cairn around the base of the standing oar.

"It is time now to make the sacrifice to your enemy Poseidon, of which Teiresias spoke," said the stranger. "I will go to the people in the valley who will give me a ram and a bull from the flocks, but you yourself must go into wild country and bring the breeding boar. I cannot help you there; but perhaps you may find him ready to come with you."

Odysseus looked at him in disbelief. "I must bring him alive," he said despairingly, "but that is surely impossible. Bow or knife cannot be used. I will take only a rope with a noose—and pray."

Odysseus took the road that led into the woods. He knew now what this sacrifice meant: three offerings of the driving power of his masculinity, which had carried him through so many trials but had also been given over to pride and ambition and greed of achievement. The ram and the bull were not hard to find and offer—but the breeding boar? That wild and dangerous beast, hidden in the forests of his soul, breeding unseen new and more deadly threats of pride—pride now in his own renunciations—how could he be tamed?

He heard a rustling in the undergrowth and stood still. All his senses, his fears, his doubts and longings, seemed to come together into a point of sheer attention beyond thought. He moved slowly to stand on a flat rock at the side of the path and

heard a sound, a kind of humming chant, and he knew in wonder that it was his own voice singing—calling to the huge boar
whose head now showed amongst the trees. Gradually the
threat in the black angry eyes sank to rest and Odysseus
dropped the rope with its noose. The huge creature emerged
slowly into sight and approached the stone. Odysseus with a
stab of fear stood without moving, then dared to turn, still
singing, and walk back along the path. He heard the heavy
plodding of the boar behind him and knew with joy, "He
comes consenting." The stranger was there as he approached
the oar: a white ram and a red bull were beside him and the
black boar quietly joined them. Together Odysseus and his
companion built three fires and, taking the ritual knife,
Odysseus shed the blood of the sacrifice, and as it poured out
he knew that the long enmity between him and the great god
Poseidon, Earthshaker and Power of the Sea, was at an end,
and that he and Polyphemos, son of the god, were one at last in
the new life in which he was unique and yet many, nothing,
and everything. He and the other ate the ritual part of the
threefold offering to the god; then Odysseus said, "I leave the
meat to the people of this place and I go now, O stranger, no
longer strange to me, to make the ceremonial offerings, as
Teiresias foretold, at home among my people." He called to his
quietly grazing donkey and looked back to say goodbye, but
the stranger had disappeared and with him all traces of the sacrifice: the oar stood tall and straight between earth and sky.

So Odysseus came home, and, day by day, he made offering
to each of the gods in turn, under their Greek names and

forms—names which differ in time and space throughout the centuries and in all the varying cultures of our world. They carry always for men and women the meanings of life, both human and divine, and in these final rites Odysseus surely affirmed the wholeness of his life's journey, his readiness to die. He made offerings to Zeus and Hera, Apollo and Artemis, Dionysus and Aphrodite, Hephaestos, Ares, Hecate, Hades, Demeter-Persephone; then came his particular gratitude to the great powers who had chiefly guided him and brought him and Penelope to their present rich serenity—grey-eyed Athene, who in dreams had given the wisdom and courage to save them both; and Hermes, who long ago had given him the herb "moli" with its black roots and milky flowers, the one protection from Circe who turned men into swine. Hermes was the one also who brought him release from Calypso and who, he now knew, had met him at the crossroads and awakened him on the threshold of old age. Last of all he remembered and gave thanks for Eros and Psyche, united after much suffering and giving birth to "Joy."

In the time that followed I imagine the old Greek living the simple life in the mode of his time, as so many, in other times and cultures who have experienced the return to innocence. It is a life, we may imagine, both wholly symbolic and yet wholly natural, empty yet full, spontaneous as a child's, yet constantly chosen. "Love and do as you will," in St. Augustine's words. Thus, as Teiresias saw, he would grow into a rich old age until, weighted with the length of years yet light as a breath of wind, death would come gently to him out of the sea.

KING LEAR

CORDELIA: For thee, oppressed king, am I cast down;
Myself could else out-frown false fortune's frown.
Shall we not see these daughters and these sisters?

LEAR: No, no, no, no! Come, let's away to prison:
We two alone will sing like birds i'the cage:
When thou dost ask me blessing, I'll kneel down
And ask of thee forgiveness: so we'll live,
And pray, and sing, and tell old tales, and laugh
At gilded butterflies, and hear poor rogues
Talk of court news; and we'll talk with them too—
Who loses and who wins; who's in, who's out—
And take upon's the mystery of things,
As if we were God's spies: and we'll wear out,
In a wall'd prison, packs and sects of great ones,
That ebb and flow by th'moon.

Surely in all the poetry of the world there could be no more profoundly beautiful, wise, and tender expression of the essence of old age, of the kind of life to which one may come in the last years if one has, like Lear, lived through and accepted all the passion and suffering, the darkness and light, the beauty and horror of one's experience of the world and of oneself.

On a first reading it is easy to miss the profundity, absorbed as we are in the drama, and see it only as a beautiful fantasy of the old man seeking peace behind actual prison walls with his beloved daughter. But on a second, third, and fourth reading, who could fail to realize the immensity of the images, and to see how little an actual dungeon has to do with the story?

Cordelia wishes to go out to meet the evil thing and confront it. Because she is young, this response is true and right. For the old, this is no longer the way—"No, no, no, no! Come, let's away to prison." As a man grows old, his body weakens, his powers fail, his sight perhaps is dimmed, his hearing fades, or his power to move around is taken from him. In one way or another he is "imprisoned," and the moment of choice will come to him. Will he fight this confining process or will he go to meet it in the spirit of King Lear—embrace it with love, with eagerness even? The wisdom of common speech, which we so often miss, speaks to us in the phrase, "He is growing old." We use it indiscriminately about those who are in truth *growing* into old age, into the final flowering and meaning of their lives, and about those who are being dragged into it, protesting, resisting, crying out against their inevitable imprisonment. Only to one who can say with his or her whole being, "Come, let's away to prison," does this essay apply.

"We two alone will sing like birds i'the cage." We may think of Cordelia in this context as the old man's inner child—the love and courage, the simplicity and innocence of his soul, to which suffering has united him. Cordelia, as Harold C. Goddard has so beautifully pointed out, while remaining an entirely human person, is also a spirit. Throughout the play she is a symbol of the innocence, the true feeling, that the king so brutally rejected, to which he so blessedly returns, and which, in the instant before death, brings to him, in a flash of vision, the full realization of immortality. So, as the bird pours out notes of joy in its cage, the old man will sing out of his pure love of life in the prison of his enforced inactivity.

Now come those two wonderful lines, "When thou dost ask me blessing, I'll kneel down and ask of thee forgiveness." If an old person does not feel his need to be forgiven by the young, he or she certainly has not grown into age, but merely fallen into it, and his or her "blessing" would be worth nothing. The lines convey with the utmost brevity and power the truth that the blessing that the old may pass on to the young springs only out of that humility that is the fruit of wholeness, the humility that knows *how* to kneel, *how* to ask forgiveness. The old man kneels, not in order to ease guilt feelings (which is at the root of so much apologizing) but in the full and free acceptance of that which Charles Williams called *co-inherence*. King Lear does not say, "I am not worthy to bless you, only to grovel at your feet." He says, "When you ask me blessing, I'll kneel...." The kneeling is the blessing.

"So we'll live," he continues. The exchange of blessings between one human being and another is the essence of life itself. "And pray, and sing, and tell old tales, and laugh at gilded butterflies...." Here are the proper occupations of old age:

1) prayer, which is the quickening of the mind, the rooting of the
2) attention in the ground of being; song, which is the expression of
3) spontaneous joy in the harmony of the chaos; the "telling of old tales," which among all primitives was the supreme function of the old, who passed on the wisdom of the ancestor through the symbol, through the understanding of the dreams of the race that their long experience had taught them. In our days how sadly lost, despised even, is the function of the old! Wisdom being identified with knowledge, the "old tale" has become the subject of learned historical research, and only for the few does it remain the carrier of true wisdom of heart and mind, of body and spirit. When the old cease to "dream dreams," to be "tellers of old tales," the time must come of which the Book of Proverbs speaks: "Where there is no vision, the people perish."

4) And laughter! Surely laughter of a certain kind springs from the heart of those who have truly grown old. It is the laughter of pure delight in beauty—beauty of which the golden butterfly is the perfect symbol—a fleeting, ephemeral thing, passing on the wind, eternally reborn from the earthbound worm, the fragile yet omnipotent beauty of the present moment.

All these four things are activities *without purpose;* any one of them is immediately killed by any hint of striving for achievement. They come to birth only in a heart freed from preoccupation with the goals of the ego, however "spiritual" or lofty these goals may be.

This, however, does not mean that in old age we are to separate ourselves from concern with the world. Without a pause, without even a new sentence, Shakespeare adds to praying, singing, the telling of tales, and laughter an image of listening—listening to the smallest concerns of those still caught in the goals of power. This kind of imprisonment is never a shutting out, a rejection. "And hear poor rogues talk of court news; and we'll talk with them too—who loses and who wins; who's in, who's out." Not only does the wise old man listen, he responds: "And we'll talk with them too." It is not a matter of listening in a superior manner to problems that the king has outgrown. We feel the smiling tenderness of that phrase "poor rogues," untainted by contempt or boredom, and we can almost hear the old king gravely answering each with his own truth, always interested and concerned, never preaching, but offering to each some glimpse of inner freedom.

There follow the few words that are the climax of the whole speech—only a line and a half—words so moving, of such shining beauty, that if they are heard in the depths of one's being, they can surely never be forgotten but will sing in one's heart for the rest of time. "And take upon's the mystery of things, as if we were God's spies." This is the final responsibility of each person's life. Will we or will we not, as we approach the prison of old age, accept this supreme task? It is not the function of the old to explain or to analyze or to impart information. To them comes the great opportunity of taking upon themselves the mystery of things, of becoming, as it were, God's spies. A spy is one who penetrates into a hidden mystery, and a spy of God is that one who sees at the heart of every manifestation of life, even behind the trivial talk of "poor rogues," the *mysterium tremendum* that is God. Explanations and information, necessary

49

as they are along the way, make clear only partial truths, and the danger of mistaking half-truths for truth itself cannot be exaggerated. We are inclined to use the word "mystery" when we are really speaking of a confused muddle or an ignorant superstition. On the contrary, the true mystery is the eternal paradox at the root of life itself—it is that which, instead of hiding truth, reveals the whole, not the part. So, when after having made every effort to understand, we are ready to take upon ourselves the mystery of things, then the most trivial of happenings is touched by wonder, and there may come to us, by grace, a moment of unclouded vision.

"And we'll wear out, in a wall'd prison, packs and sects of great ones, that ebb and flow by th'moon." "In a wall'd prison" the spirit of the king is free, while those who think they have made themselves great through the instinctive greed of the pack, through fanatical assertion of the rights of sects or party, are the truly imprisoned. They are the ones at the mercy of the ebb and flow of the unconscious forces they despise. The king himself had been one of these "great ones," driven by his lust for flattery, blind to all individual feeling values, dominated by the ebb and flow of the moon, the unconscious, undifferentiated feminine within. But now, at the end, the storm of his suffering has transmuted the lust and cruelty of the pack, of the mob, into tenderness and compassion, has swept away the blind sectarian judgments of his vanity, leaving him alone, a free individual with his Cordelia, his innocence reborn.

"We'll wear out the packs and sects. . . ." What a cry of hope—more than that—of certainty for the human spirit in this world of totalitarian values! One man alone, embracing his prison, reborn into innocence, can "outwear" their terrifying power, not only through patience and suffering, but through prayer and song and laughter and telling of old tales. The rocket and the bomb can never at the last prevail over the golden butterfly. This was Shakespeare's ultimate certainty. "How with this rage shall beauty hold a plea, whose action is no stronger than a flower?"[7] How indeed? And yet it does, he answers in his greatest plays, notably in the miraculous ending of *King Lear.*

Into these twelve brief lines, spoken by an old man of eighty, Shakespeare has condensed all the essential wisdom into which we may hope to grow in our closing years, but they do not speak only to the very old. At every age, in every person, there comes a partial imprisonment, a disabling psychic wound, an unavoidable combination of circumstances, a weakness that we cannot banish, but must simply accept. Necessity in all its forms imprisons us, and if we could always with a single heart say to our own Cordelias, "Come, let's away to prison: we two alone will sing like birds i'the cage," the confining walls would become the alchemist's retort. Inside this retort we would "take upon's the mystery of things," and so the base metal would be transmuted into gold.

How clumsy at the last seem all these words—indeed all words that purport to explain or illuminate great poetry! Yet often we need them to awaken our dulled perception; we speak and hear them in order that we may turn from them again and let the poetry itself speak to us out of silence.

No, no, no, no! Come, let's away to prison:
We two alone will sing like birds i'the cage:
When thou dost ask me blessing, I'll kneel down
And ask of thee forgiveness. So we'll live,
And pray, and sing, and tell old tales, and laugh
At gilded butterflies, and hear poor rogues
Talk of court news; and we'll talk with them too—
Who loses and who wins; who's in, who's out—
And take upon's the mystery of things,
As if we were God's spies: and we'll wear out,
In a wall'd prison, packs and sects of great ones,
That ebb and flow by th'moon.

King Lear 5.3.8–19

THE TEMPEST

Re: forgiveness
its salvation

SHAKESPEARE IN *The Tempest*, his last great play, has left us images of a *rite de passage* that may arouse questions and awaken intuitions of meaning hidden in the years already lived in time, and point forward to the changes of attitude which must come to us if we are to seek a deeper and more conscious approach to death in our later years.

The Tempest is above all a play about transformations. King Alonso, Ferdinand, Miranda, Caliban—all of them change in the play; but these changes are a kind of expansion, a consequence of the transformation of the aging Prospero himself as he approaches the moment when he will set Ariel free.

It has been truly said that *The Tempest* is a play whose innumerable meanings can never be caught or analyzed, for every time it is read it speaks with a different voice to each individual reader. Indeed, on that same reader its impact changes with each new reading—and particularly at different phases of his growth into maturity and old age. This of course is true only for those who continue to *grow* old and do not merely sink into the aging process or attempt to delay it. Anything that is written about *The Tempest* must therefore be heard as the response of one individual to the poet's vision; it can never be claimed as collectively valid. But the impact on one may also awaken in another his or her own unique response.

The question is—and it is a burning question in the sense that, once asked, the fire of it burns on, or smoulders, in the mind—what does it mean for a man or woman approaching death to set free the Ariel in himself—to break the staff and drown the book? In order to find an answer an individual must seek in the unconscious for his or her own image of an Ariel—that "tricksy spirit"—and recreate him in imagination until his reality in the psyche is recognized. First, however, let us watch the pattern of Prospero's life and seek to intuit the meaning of Ariel in him.

When the play opens we are shown Prospero at the height of his creative powers and we then watch the drama of the events that immediately precede his final "letting go." We are also, however, given a clear backward look at his early life when (in act I, scene 2) after raising the storm that brought his enemies into his power, he tells his daughter, Miranda, for the first time, the story of their coming to the island when she was still too young to remember.

We learn that he had been Duke of Milan, but that gradually he had handed over more and more of the business of governing to his brother, Antonio, preferring to spend his time and energy on research and study with a special emphasis on secret lore—the occult, as it would be called today. His wife was dead; the feminine absent in his life. He was blind to people as well as to facts, and he altogether failed to see what manner of man his brother was or to recognize his own share of the responsibility for what happened. Antonio, his brother, became avid for power—a clear image of Prospero's own shadow; for we clearly see the love of power of another kind that possesses Prospero in the play.

In those days of his youth in Milan, Antonio had made a pact with the King of Naples, and together they plotted the death of Prospero—not by direct murder but by sending him out to sea in a leaky boat with his three-year-old daughter, Miranda. But his old friend, the kindly Gonzalo, placed food and clothing and his precious books ("that I prize above my dukedom") on board and so gave him a chance to survive, and thus he came with his baby daughter to his enchanted island.

We may see in this story the truth that however blind, unbalanced, and dangerously one-sided a man or woman may be in youth, he will be saved by the one essential quality of the inner life—devotion. It must be, of course, a devotion to something beyond the ego, something that he loves with real integrity without counting the cost, as Prospero loved the study of his books. This object of devotion will carry for him, for the time being, a projection of his hidden and often quite unconscious awareness of the Self. Charles Williams has unforgettably expressed this truth in these few words: "Unless devotion is given to a thing that must prove false in the end, the thing that is true in the end cannot enter."[8]

Prospero, then, was not destroyed psychically or physically by his blindness to his own shadow side or his neglect of the values of the heart; his capacity for devotion was a measure of his capacity for growth into wholeness, and he was saved by the warm heart of his friend Gonzalo. Therefore his destiny led him, after his confrontation with danger and with the physical hardships of his voyage at the mercy of wind and storm, to that magic island—that *temenos* in the unconscious where an individual, through long years of inner work, may at last find his way to the self-knowledge which is the City of God.[9]

Prospero was precipitated by what seemed to him an evil fate for which, at that time, he felt in no way responsible ("that a brother should be so perfidious") into the absolute necessity of bringing up his inferior and neglected qualities.

Thrust out to sea, at the mercy of the elements, he was forced to take care not only of his own physical needs (things he must always have had servants to do for him) but, most important of all, had to bring up his feminine feeling and care in all the most basic ways for a three-year-old daughter—care like a mother as well as a father. That he immediately responded to the challenge is shown to us in the tenderness of his reply to Miranda, when she exclaimed "Alack, what trouble was I then to you!" and he replies,

> O, a cherubin
> Thou wast that did preserve me! Thou didst smile,
> Infused with a fortitude from heaven,
> When I have deck'd the sea with drops full salt,
> Under my burden groan'd; which raised in me
> An undergoing stomach, to bear up
> Against what should ensue.

Then, ending his story,

> Sit still, and hear the last of our sea-sorrow.
> Here in this island we arrived; and here
> Have I, thy schoolmaster, made thee more profit
> Than other princes can, that have more time
> For vainer hours, and tutors not so careful.

He is still full of pride about the gifts of his mind to her, but her wonderful innocence and trust reveal to her clearly his truly sensitive feeling side. Miranda has grown to womanhood, image of his own slowly maturing soul.

She sleeps now after this revelation of their history and, Prospero having donned his wizard's robe, we are immediately introduced to that unique, indescribable being, whom Prospero calls "my Ariel."

Hear Ariel's first words about himself (though neither "he," "she," nor "it" are accurate pronouns):

> All hail, great master! grave sir, hail! I come
> To answer thy best pleasure; be't to fly,
> To swim, to drive into the fire, to ride
> On the curl'd clouds—to thy strong bidding task
> Ariel and all his quality.

He had come raising, at Prospero's bidding, the great storm that had brought the ship with all his enemies onboard to Prospero's island.

I boarded the king's ship; now on the beak,
Now in the waist, the deck, in every cabin,
I flamed amazement: sometime I'd divide,
And burn in many places; on the topmast,
The yards, and bowsprit, would I flame distinctly,
Then meet, and join.

He goes on to say that the lightning surpassed Jove's in swiftness, and the roaring of the sea equaled Neptune's fury. He is a spirit of fire, of air, of wind, of water—"to fly, to swim, to ride the curl'd clouds"—and he brings all the sufferers at last to walk on the solid earth in safety. He is that spirit in all of us that brings to birth—to incarnation—the creative imagination. Years earlier Shakespeare had written: "The lunatic, the lover and the poet are of imagination all compact."[10] And Wordsworth wrote in *The Prelude:*

> Imagination, which, in truth
> Is but another name for absolute power
> And clearest insight, amplitude of mind
> And Reason in her most exalted mood.

If this absolute power of the imagination overwhelms a man's reason, drowning his ego-consciousness so that, in Jung's words, there is nobody there to give it form, it creates the lunatic. In the lover it is experienced first in projection, and may lead either to possession by ego-centered desire, or to the ever-growing consciousness of the love and compassion that transcend emotion; but it is the poet's eye in each of us that "glances from heaven to earth, from earth to heaven." And

> . . . as imagination bodies forth
> The forms of things unknown, the poet's pen
> Turns them to shapes and gives to airy nothing
> A local habitation and a name.[11]

There are very few who wield the true poet's pen in the literal sense, but the poet's eye is there for all who know wonder[12] and who work to discover in themselves the "pen" which creates "the local habitation and the name." These may take innumerable forms, different in every individual, but always there is the same fundamental task—to give form and reality in this world, in each person's actual life, to that which the "poet's eye" has seen in heaven and on earth. And this can only be through "clearest insight, amplitude of mind, and Reason in her most exalted mood." Moreover there is no amplitude of "mind" as distinct from "intellect" without largeness of heart; Wordsworth's "reason" is certainly not that of the pure intellectual.

When Prospero landed on the island he found himself alone except for an ugly creature called Caliban, son of an evil witch who had died before his arrival. Ariel was also there, but confined in a cloven pine tree by a spell of this same witch and groaning in misery. Through his long devotion to the study of the numinous, Prospero was able to release this spirit, whom he bound to his service in return for that freedom. Ariel obviously is not a simple image of Prospero's magical powers over his environment. He has existed in this island of the inner world long before Prospero, the white magician, and before Sycorax, the black witch, find him there, and both of these are human beings in exile from their outer worlds. Moreover, it is plain that he is not simply an impersonal, amoral power in the unconscious. He has been imprisoned precisely by reason of his refusal to obey the evil will of Sycorax. He is freed by Prospero and in return for his release he has consented to serve the good will of Prospero.

Perhaps we can feel Ariel as an elusive image, that no words can capture, of the spirit that Jung spoke of with caution but with increasing certainty as an unknown "something" in the unconscious, which seems to urge every individual through dreams, through synchronistic events, whenever he touches the realm of the archetypes, towards greater consciousness; and when the time approaches for the final "letting go" preceding the experience of death, he begins to urge the ego towards it by pressing for his freedom again. His function would seem to be to serve the ego by enabling it to bring to fruition in this world his image-making power—through an art of any activity undertaken with devotion; and he will also, it seems, bring, through his transforming fire, in every such person, an awareness of the major turning points of his or her life and the dangers of avoiding them. He will never bind himself to consciousness-destroying Sycorax; only to one whom, no matter what his mistakes and backslidings, is committed in the ground of his being to the quest for a truth beyond the ego's limited vision.

In their first scene together Ariel reminds Prospero that he has promised to release him from his service. Not yet, not quite yet, replies his master. His enemies are wandering about on the island on which, through Ariel, he has come to wield power over the elements themselves and feels himself as powerful as God. He uses both Ariel and Caliban—the opposite potentialities in his nature—as we all do on our way to self-knowledge. His humanity is saved and nourished only by his love and care for Miranda.

Now he must face at last the great test to which all men and women come. Will he willingly and with full consent let go of his will to power when the moment arrives, as it does, at the height of his success? His enemies are all at his mercy; he can conjure up visions and spells from the unconscious to control the lives of others for good or ill. He is faced with a supreme opportunity and a choice involving the ultimate danger of a hubris that brings total destruction.

That Prospero is half aware of both the opportunity and the danger is clear from the beginning. The fact that he has promised to let Ariel go free before the play opens sounds like a kind of assurance he is clinging to ahead of the consent of his will—an assurance to himself that he *will* have the courage to live without the powers that he has spent a lifetime building up in himself. But, like St. Augustine at his great turning point, "not yet, not quite yet," he repeats.

As always, the "not yet," while it remains a weakness of the ego, is nevertheless, as long as the deeper promise holds true, an essential part of the pattern of his growth. In the "acausal orderedness" (Jung's phrase), the "synchronicity" of the incarnation of the Self, the moment of full consent comes only when the individual suddenly awakens to the fundamental roots of his shadow projections and accepts them all. In other words, it is the breakthrough of forgiveness, in its most profound sense—universal and particular, impersonal and personal—that alone brings the "letting go," the ultimate freedom of the spirit. For in the moment of that realization, every false guilt, whether seen as one's own or as other people's, is gone forever—and the real guilt which each of us carries, of refusal to see, to be aware, is accepted. So we may look open-eyed at ourselves and the world and suffer the pain and joy of the divine conflict which is the human condition, the meaning of incarnation.

forgiveness

"Forgive us ... as we forgive ..." we may say glibly for most of our lives, whether in these words or others, explicit or vague, with small understanding of the universality of this condition. It is no accident that Shakespeare's last three great plays—*Cymbeline, The Winter's Tale,* and *The Tempest*—are all centered on the final redeeming power of forgiveness. They are Shakespeare's own testimony to the meaning of his incomparable insights into the conflicts of good and evil, and, more profoundly, of good with good in the human soul. Forgiveness is not the comfortable, often somewhat superior, "I forgive you" that comes so easily to human lips when emotions have cooled. Things are then smoothed over, but the resentment descends into the unconscious together with a hidden condition that the "forgiven" injury shall not be repeated. The ultimate experience of forgiveness brings a change of heart, a *metanoia* of the spirit, after which every seeming injury, injustice, rejection, past, present or future, every so-called blow of fate, becomes, as it were, an essential note in the music of God, however discordant it may sound to our superficial hearing. And the experience excludes nothing—which means that in this moment of forgiveness all one's sins and weaknesses are included, being at the same time both remembered and known as the essential darkness which has revealed to us the light.

Dante describes the experience of remorse and repentance in his confrontation with his shadow when at the threshold of the Earthly Paradise he meets Beatrice and she shows him the darkness in his life. All his sins are washed away and are forgotten in the river Lethe, but this indeed is not enough—it is not yet forgiveness. He must still drink of the waters of Eunoe— the spring of true knowing from which two rivers flow into the world. After this all the darkness, the weakness, and the sin is again remembered but experienced with joy as essential to his wholeness. Only then can he begin his last journey into the Paradiso towards the center where the final unity will be revealed to him. *The Tempest* is a story of the slow discovery by a highly gifted individual of the true nature of forgiveness.

To return now to Ariel and to his meaning. The minute we try to think of him in general terms, as representing this or that, we feel almost a sense of guilt—as though one had laid a heavy hand on something so fragile, so tender and elusive, unique and indefinable, that his meaning dies under our touch. This guilt I felt after writing of him a few pages back. Let it stand as a hint and a warning. William Blake speaks this truth:

He who bends to himself a joy
Doth the winged life destroy;
But he who kisses the joy as it flies
Dwells in eternity's sunrise.

Ariel himself remains unique. He is Prospero's image—and beyond that Shakespeare's personification of that which lay behind the glory of his own poetic genius. In each of us such an image lives to be released—then bound in a new sense for the time during which the ego must take up responsibility for his fiery activity in our lives, and at last be set wholly free when the time comes. There is no life at all that does not spring from the images within, and the poet in us may create through anything we do in this world, however seemingly dull. Charles Williams pointed out that only when we have taken up full responsibility for our actions do we reach the moment when all responsibility is lifted from us, if we are ready to let go.

A week before he died, Thomas Merton wrote of his experience in the garden of the Three Stone Buddhas in Ceylon. "I was jerked out of the habitual half-tied vision of things. . . ." He felt a peace filled with every possibility in which he questioned nothing any more. It was, he says, not the peace of emotional resignation but of having "seen through every question without trying to discredit anyone of anything—without refutation, without establishing some other argument."[13] His staff was broken, his book drowned, his Ariel free in this moment. He had carried his responsibility with ultimate devotion through all the ups and downs and half-tied attitudes, and the end of his life was near.

Surely, before this final enlightenment, he had experienced, as all men and women on the inner journey must, the extremes of both meaning and meaninglessness—the agonies of the approach to this moment of breakthrough which *The Tempest* reveals to us in Shakespeare's imagery.

Each of us in unique ways passes through the danger of "bending" to ourselves for too long this gift of Ariel's power. The fact that we do not feel ourselves to be faintly like the wizard with his power to control storms, enchant people, call up spirits, etc., does not affect the truth that the most unconscious and apparently "weak" people may, through their unrecognized unconscious fantasies (Ariel being still imprisoned in his tree in the unconscious) influence their environment, so to speak, "magically," in a more damaging way even than those who consciously use such creative power as they have for the ends which they conceive to be desirable. We all have magical powers operating in us and influencing our environment—and they cease to be magical slowly through our lives insofar as we are able to see and recreate these unconscious images with the "poet's eye"—whether we are artists or writers or in whatever capacity we work in the outer world, however simple. From magical powers the images may through conscious work and sacrifice be transformed into creative living of the symbolic life, which leads us to self-knowledge and glimpses of the "coinherence" (Charles Williams's word) of all things.

The first breakthrough to a realization of a meaning in one's life—the conscious discovery of the work one loves to do—may come early, often even in childhood, or much later. The recognition of a skill, or an ability to "create" in one sphere or another, may be compared to the discovery of one's own Ariel— that gift which we recognize as inborn and not learned, and which we then proceed, if we are ready to give it the necessary devotion, to set free from its prison in the unconscious, as Prospero released Ariel from the tree. We may now develop our gift through the discipline and work which we direct to our "calling," to that from which our conscious goals emerge. The outer forms of this "calling" may change often, even dramatically, along the way, but the root remains the same. Ariel will create or destroy in obedience to these goals—and the task of the middle years is the journey whereby we uncover the differing motives behind our various activities and realize how they are conditioned by the hidden fantasy life in the unconscious. It is only when these fantasies have finally become clear to us, revealing perhaps motives of egocentric power drives and greed, that we shall be able to accept and forgive both ourselves and others and set free the Ariel who has served us so faithfully through the years. He will have brought us finally to this point of self-knowledge at which it becomes possible to break the staff of power and drown the magic book of spells.

When this moment comes, all too often it may itself be refused, unrecognized. Ariel is held on to—the "winged life" is destroyed and the possibility of growth into death recedes. There may follow a desperate effort to hold on to youth and the past, to arrest the flow of the river of life as it approaches the ocean of eternity, or else the apathy of meaninglessness that Prospero feared may invade the psyche. So old age becomes decay, not in the natural sense of the cycle of life and death but in the negative and horrible sense of disintegration and despair. The superficial interpretation of Prospero's setting free of Ariel and breaking his staff as Shakespeare's personal decision to write no more plays, no more poetry, entirely misses the point. Rather it is Prospero's total acceptance of his own truth, including all his hitherto rejected darkness. With this comes the giving up of any identification with that power which has been incarnate in his life and which he has hitherto known largely through his will to use it.[14]

Prospero is approaching the moment of choice; his danger and his opportunity become increasingly clear throughout the play. Only through accepting time is time conquered, said T. S. Eliot; only after full confrontation with our own darkness, through fighting for our own truth and the taking up of responsibility for it may we finally be set free to live "without refutation" in the forgiveness that "discredits nothing"—in the Mercy. All these things are foreshadowed, as we shall see, in the epilogue to *The Tempest*.

As has been said, Prospero has used his magic powers to bring his enemies, through a shipwreck, into his power. It is clear that he has two motives—one to bring his beloved daughter into contact with Ferdinand, the son of the King of Naples, hoping that if the young man proves worthy, they will fall in love and that she will find happiness in marriage with him and a return to the world. But overshadowing this there is the will to take revenge on those who had so greatly injured him. It is obvious that he has no very clearly thought-out purpose. It appears that he has no intent to kill them, but seems to be reveling in playing tricks on them, more to show off his magic powers and frighten them than with any coherent plan. He also evokes and makes visible to Ferdinand and Miranda a pageant of goddesses which, in spite of its lofty themes, is largely a display of his powers. It is while he is engaged in these things that he almost forgets the danger in which he stands from the plots of Caliban to murder him. Indeed this points most clearly to the working of his hidden and unacknowledged Caliban-like nature in the tricks he is forcing Ariel to play on his old enemies while he is absorbed in his pageants.

If Ariel is the spirit of air and fire, Caliban is his dark opposite, the heavy earth of Prospero's psyche, which his intellect and his great intuition have despised and rejected. Caliban is the son of the witch—the rejected, devouring feminine image in Shakespeare's time as in ours. Prospero makes much of how "good" he was to Caliban in early years, teaching him how to speak his language, trying to civilize him, etc. But there is a sense of condescension throughout, an attitude of "I'll turn him into a useful slave"—rather than a respect for his earthiness and his potential value as an individual—and it seems to have taken Prospero completely by surprise when Caliban finally tries to possess Miranda by violence. Her father could have expected it. We may ask ourselves what was going on in Prospero's own repressed instinctual life for which Caliban was a projection point; but from the consequences of this repression he is saved precisely by the growing truth and selflessness of his love for his daughter—his willingness to use all his powers to find her a way back to humanity through a lover of true integrity who will, as he knows, take her away from him. That this intention takes precedence over all his thoughts of revenge is made very clear in the early scenes with Ariel, Ferdinand, and Miranda.

Nevertheless, Caliban remains rejected, enslaved, and cowed by fear into Prospero's service—and in his moment of greatest danger of spirit, the wizard is very near to being murdered by that instinctive creature of earth, who longs in his heart for a vision of beauty and true divinity to worship. Finding nothing but total contempt in his master, he projects his desire onto the drunken butler Stephano, who is uplifted by quite another version of spirit! How great is Shakespeare's genius to evoke for a moment in a few lines of great poetry that potential beauty hidden behind Caliban's brutish and ugly appearance and behavior:

Be not afear'd; the isle is full of noises,
Sounds, and sweet airs, that give delight and hurt not.
Sometimes a thousand twanging instruments
Will hum about mine ears; and sometimes voices
That, if I then had waked after long sleep
Will make me sleep again; and then, in dreaming,
The clouds, methought, would open and show riches
Ready to drop upon me; that when I waked
I cried to dream again.[15]

But Prospero turns all this to torment for Caliban, who decides his master must therefore be destroyed. The lines come immediately after talk of murder and are followed at once by a return to such thoughts.

Immersed in his magic pageant, Prospero has forgotten all about that dark threat, and even Ariel says he was afraid to interrupt his master's pleasure and remind him. When he suddenly remembers "that foul conspiracy of the beast Caliban," all the spirits "heavily vanish" "to a strange, hollow and confused noise,"[16] and it is now that he speaks the famous line about all images dissolving into nothing. For an instant the veil lifts for him and reality begins to break through the hubris in which he is caught. He admits to the weakness of his aging experience—"my old brain is troubled." This is the first hint that Prospero is an old man and weakening. But then with Ariel at his command, calling him "my bird" and praising him for having tormented Caliban and his companions, he sends him to play more tricks on them and calls Caliban a "born devil"— "I will plague them all even to roaring." "At this hour lie at my mercy all my enemies." The moment of vision has not yet come, but it is very near—and with it the realization that he himself must plead for mercy.

The fifth act opens with Prospero's words:

PROSPERO: Now doth my project gather to a head;
My charms crack not; my spirits obey; and time
Goes upright with his carriage. How's the day?
ARIEL: On the sixth hour; at which time, my lord,
You said our work should cease.
PROSPERO: I did say so,
When first I raised the tempest. Say, my spirit,
How fares the king and's followers?

The moment has arrived. There can be no more putting off. "I did say so." He addresses Ariel directly as "my spirit," whom he has hitherto regarded as his own, to whom he has promised freedom at this hour—and Ariel's first wholly free word it is that awakens Prospero to simple humanity as a value greater than all his wizardry.

Ariel describes the miserable, distressed state of the king and all his companions, held motionless by a spell, prisoners of Prospero's will, and he speaks of the good old lord Gonzalo. "His tears run down his beard. . . ." "If you now beheld them, your affections would have become tender."

PROSPERO: Dost thou think so, spirit? [not "my spirit"]
ARIEL: Mine would sir, were I human.
PROSPERO: And mine shall.
Hast thou, which art but air, a touch, a feeling
Of their afflictions? and shall not myself,
One of their kind, that relish all as sharply
Passion as they, be kindlier moved than thou art?

Passion is transmuted into compassion.

. . . Go release them, Ariel:
My charms I'll break, their senses I'll restore,
And they shall be themselves.

Note that he does not say "they shall be what I want them to be" after this experience.

Left alone, Prospero repeats to himself with a last surge of pride all the wonders of his power over nature and man, and even over the dead.

> . . . But this rough magic
> I here abjure . . .
> . . . I'll break my staff,
> Bury it certain fathoms in the earth,
> And deeper than did ever plummet sound
> I'll drown my book.

The way is open for that total forgiveness in which, I believe, Shakespeare conveys to us his own final vision of the ultimate meaning of redemption and wholeness. As Gonzalo sums it up—on that island, "All of us have found ourselves when no man was his own." Each of them has learned, in his degree, the utter powerlessness of his personal will, and so, for the moment anyway, has glimpsed his innermost self just as it is.

But it is not until the very end that we can quite believe in Prospero's awakening, nor be sure that his new state of forgiveness is of the nature of redemption. Ariel has sung his song of freedom—"Merrily, merrily shall I live now . . ." but he does one more thing willingly for Prospero, who asks him to "untie the spell," to set Caliban free. And then as all are gathered before his cell and the high words of forgiving have been spoken, Prospero calls to Caliban, "this demi-devil," son of the witch, and says clearly and irrevocably, "This thing of darkness I acknowledge mine."

Caliban, after an obviously astonished moment, is now himself, through being accepted, transformed from a blind slave consumed by hatred to a willing servant.

> . . . and I'll be wise hereafter,
> And seek for grace. What a thrice-double ass
> Was I to take this drunkard for a god,
> And worship this dull fool!

It is the final test—the realization of the Caliban in ourselves, rejected and seeking false gods, and the clearly spoken, "This too is I." There can be no true forgiving of another without this taking up of responsibility for the darkness and ugliness that is ours. And here I quote a passage of great beauty from Laurens van der Post's autobiography:

> As I lay there watching Kaspersen, my mind turned again to the last self-portrait by Rembrandt. To me it remains an almost unbearably moving testament, wherein the painter bequeaths the totality of himself impartially to all who have eyes to see. And the emphasis must be on the totality, because gone at last are all the special pleadings, evasions and excuses that men use to blind themselves to the whole truth of themselves, discovering in the process their portion of the estate of aboriginal darkness to which they are the natural heirs and successors. . . . Yet, no matter how much greater the defects revealed, there is at last, unblurred in those blood-streaked old eyes, a look of a certainty of pardon,

and an intimation that through total surrender to the truth of himself he has been emancipated from error and discovered something greater than even his art to carry him on beyond the advancing moment when painting would end.[17]

The last words of the play are Prospero's to Ariel:

. . . My Ariel—chick—
That is thy charge: then to the elements
Be free, and fare thou well!

The play is over: the story of Prospero's life—of the stuff upon which dreams have been made—has been told by the poet whose inner eye can "glance from heaven to earth, from earth to heaven." But Prospero does not leave the stage with his final consent to the ending of his exercise of power in the sphere of being that has held the greatest meaning for him. He has been given back his position of leadership in human affairs, but he is afraid. He stands outside the story of his life; alone as he has never been alone before, even in his first experience of exile; and he speaks to the audience in the dark auditorium as though to the "other" in every man and woman—that true "other" whom we touch in all our meetings when once we have become capable of standing alone.

"Please you," says Prospero to us all, "draw near," and he speaks the epilogue.

Now my charms are all o'erthrown,
And what strength I have's mine own—

Which is most faint: now, 'tis true,
I must be here confined by you,
Or sent to Naples. Let me not,
Since I have my dukedom got,
And pardon'd the deceiver, dwell
In this bare island by your spell;
But release me from my bands
With the help of your good hands:
Gentle breath of yours my sails
Must fill, or else my project fails,
Which was to please: Now I want
Spirits to enforce, art to enchant;
And my ending is despair,
Unless I be relieved by prayer,
Which pierces so, that it assaults
Mercy itself, and frees all faults.
As you from crimes would pardon'd be,
Let your indulgence set me free.

On the Elizabethan stage epilogues were a common way for the dramatist to ask for applause, and this final epilogue of Shakespeare's can carry this meaning on the surface, but we must not forget Shakespeare's way of speaking on more than one level at once. It is surely impossible, if one listens at all to the last six lines, to ignore the depth of their meaning in the "ground" of the psyche.

In this epilogue, we are made aware of a startling paradox. The moment of letting go, of daring to stand alone, stripped of

the task of Age

77

power and prestige, bereft of any sense of worth or superior knowledge, is at the same time the moment when such a man or woman becomes conscious of his absolute need of "the other" both in this world and in the Beyond. A choice between two ways then lies ahead. We may either continue in our last years to cling to our past achievements and worn-out values, thus sinking eventually into complete dependence on others, on collective opinions, demands, and attitudes; or we may confront our growing weakness and loss of energy, together with our past rejections, sins, and blindness (the "Caliban" within), and so approach that kind of free dependence on "the other" which brings us to the meaning of forgiveness and to kinship with all things.

kinship + interdependence. The experience of this kinship, this unity, has been described by great poets, artists, and mystics of all ages; and in our own century have been added the voices not only of the psychologists but finally of the quantum physicists themselves, exploring the subatomic world. The reality of all life is, as it were, an unceasing dance on all levels of being, material, instinctual, psychic, and spiritual, in which every motion of the tiniest part, weaving patterns of exchange and transformation, affects the whole. It goes on in the particles of the material universe, in the lives of plants, insects, animals, in the eating and being eaten which maintain the balance of life and death in nature, in the play of opposites in the unconscious psyche; and finally, since the dawn of consciousness, it seems that there is a mystery at the center of all these movements of the dance which has, in the dimension of linear time, always pressed up from below, down from above, to awaken in individual human beings a growing awareness of *meaning*. Then a recognition of the patterns of the dance becomes possible in our own lives, an intuition of the interdependence of each with all, which is at the same time the gateway to freedom of spirit and the sunrise of eternity. There is no private salvation; exchange with the other is the door to the final awareness of the unity of all in the love which is the dance of creation.

Here I shall quote two profound declarations of this truth. In the imagery of the fourteenth century, medieval anchoress Julian of Norwich writes:

> When Adam fell, God's son fell: because of the rightful oneing wich had been made in heven, God's Son might not [be disparted] from Adam. (For by Adam I understand All-Man.) . . . God's Son fell with Adam, into the deep of the Maiden's womb. . . .[18]

This is a symbol beyond cause and effect. Man's choice of consciousness—the knowledge of good and evil—was simultaneously God's choice of incarnation, death, and resurrection to the eternity of love. "O happy fault, that wert the occasion for so great a redemption."[19]

The second quotation is from the end of Jung's autobiography, *Memories, Dreams, Reflections*. It was rare for him to write directly about love and of our dependence on it, but in his old age he poured into this one beautiful paragraph the intensity of his experience of this truth.

On "love"

Here is the greatest and smallest, the remotest and nearest, the highest and lowest, and we cannot discuss one side of it without also discussing the other. No language is adequate to this paradox. Whatever one can say, no words express the whole. . . . Love "bears all things" and "endures all things" (1 Cor. 13:7). These words say all there is to be said; nothing can be added to them. For we are in the deepest sense the victims and instruments of cosmogonic "love." I put the word in quotation marks to indicate that I do not use it in its connotations of desiring, preferring, favoring, wishing, and similar feelings, but as something superior to the individual, a unified and undivided whole. Being a part, man cannot grasp the whole. He is at its mercy. He may assent to it, or rebel against it; but he is always caught up by it and enclosed within it. He is dependent upon it and sustained by it. Love is his light and his darkness, whose end he cannot see. "Love ceases not"— whether he speaks with the "tongue of angels," or with scientific exactitude traces the life of the cell down to its uttermost source. Man can try to name love, showering upon it all the names at his command, and still he will involve himself in endless self-deceptions. If he possesses a grain of wisdom, he will lay down his arms and name the unknown by the more unknown, "ignotum per ignotius"—that is, by the name of God. That is a confession of his subjection, his imperfection, and his dependence; but at the same time a testimony to his freedom to choose between truth and error.[20]

Prospero, like anyone who has had an Ariel at his command, had glimpsed these things "as through a glass, darkly," for the use of magic is precisely a manipulation of such intuitive knowledge of the realities beyond cause and effect. Mystics and occultists, sibyls and clairvoyants alike have acquired such powers, and all those who have been true visionaries of love have pointed out their dangers if *used* by the ego, even with the highest-seeming motives, to serve goals that seem to the human reason unquestionably "good."

Prospero has now renounced his spell-making powers; and, hardest of all, he has set Ariel free. He now must face the inevitable experience, one way or another, of those who are nearing the end of their lives. All these powers will be taken from us anyway in the fulfilling of the pattern of life and death; but there is an enormous difference, as has been said, between the man who, as it were, "creates" his inevitable fate by a clear choice made with total assent, and one who is drawn into the changes of "the dance" resisting and clinging to the past. For this kind of person the "book" is not drowned—rather he himself is in danger of drowning in the undifferentiated unconscious.

This danger, especially for a highly creative individual, is clearly stated by Shakespeare in Prospero's epilogue. "Now I want [that is, 'lack'] spirits to enforce, arts to enchant, and my ending is despair, unless. . . ." This comes near the end of the epilogue and we shall return to what follows these words. The beginning of the epilogue is a description of the state of mind from which only "the other" can release him—the state of mind which can hold a man imprisoned until he sinks into despair.

Outwardly this makes no sense. At the end of the play all is clear and set fair for the journey home to Italy. But suddenly here is the old man clearly saying that he will have to remain on "this bare island" trapped by a spell as he had entrapped others, unless he is set free by those who have truly responded to his story in their hearts. It is altogether too superficial to interpret this simply as Shakespeare asking his audiences not to demand any more plays from him. He was obviously far too enlightened to have been in any danger of despair from such outer demands. The peril with which Prospero was threatened and which his creator must have known, was something altogether more subtle. No longer could he summon the spirit Ariel at will; instead he must take responsibility for the "Caliban" whom he had for so long despised and rejected (I use the biblical words advisedly)— and to him the threat lay in a great fear that he himself would never escape from a kind of imprisonment in the awful boredom of his enchanted island, deprived of all that had given it meaning and beauty. His body might return to the cities of men where he would be surrounded by family, friends, courtiers, but he knew that he might remain inwardly imprisoned on an island now become a desert for him, because for so long he had lived by his magical powers through the enslavement of Ariel and Caliban. How dull might he find the ordinary human contacts of life now—"how weary, stale, flat, and unprofitable"—compared to the casting of spells over people and to the glory of his visions of the gods!

At the end of the play itself he had said that henceforth every third thought of his would be of his grave. But that, in old age, may be a sign of the very opposite of despair, arising from the growing recognition of death as woven into the fabric of any life that has meaning; indeed such frequent attention to the meaning of death may be the way to final release from the shadow of despair. Having made that remark about death he bids Ariel see to giving the ships "calm seas, auspicious gales." Then with a great gesture of release and farewell he stands stripped of all his powers, suddenly face to face with the realization of what lies before him, and of what it really means to forgive and be forgiven and so to be ready to die.

In W. H. Auden's poem "The Sea and the Mirror," which is about the characters in *The Tempest* after the events of the play, the poet imagines Prospero saying to Ariel, "I am glad that I have freed you, so at last I can really believe I shall die. For under your influence death is inconceivable." To be *unable* to conceive the reality of death is not at all the same thing as "living in eternity's sunrise." This is only a possibility when Ariel is free.

Looking back at the forgiveness scenes of the play, we may detect Prospero's relatively superficial first expressions of the forgiveness to which Ariel has opened his heart. It is still the "good," superior, injured man speaking to sinners—especially when he says to Antonio, "You, most wicked Sir, whom to call brother would infect my mouth, I do forgive thy rankest fault." That kind of self-righteous forgiveness will never bring the forgiveness of which he later, in the epilogue, discovers his own need. We can follow the stages of his growing awareness. The King of Naples with a touching humility, after discovering

Ferdinand and Miranda, pledged to each other in joy, and accepting her as a daughter, says, "O, how oddly will it sound that I must ask my child forgiveness!" Prospero obviously would rather not look at things of that nature yet. "There sir, stop: let us not burden our remembrances with a heaviness that's gone." It was probably good advice to Alonso at the moment. But he will soon know that for himself it remains to be endured.

Gonzalo now turns away from Prospero's magical surprises as he expresses his thanks to the gods for the outcome of all their good and evil fortune, including Prospero's; he rejoices that "in a poor isle" all of them have found themselves, "when no man was his own." Here we may imagine that the wisdom of Prospero's heart speaks to him, and it is after this that the real inner change begins. Now he sets Caliban free—but knows himself bound—bound to his own rejected human weakness.

After the immediate responses to the play itself, varying in intensity and in meaning with each individual, it is easy for many people in Shakespeare's "audience" to dismiss the epilogue as a mere appendage to which they listen with only a fraction of their attention. But as a lover of the play grows older, it begins to speak with a louder and much more urgent voice, and its paradoxes enter the psyche with questions to which experience and love and reflection together must bring to each his answer.

At this point, it may be objected that I have been talking of the dangers that threaten in old age, but that Shakespeare was not an old man when he wrote these lines. It should therefore be added that this kind of experience, it appears, comes to those who, although comparatively young in years, have lived their lives with great intensity of devotion and whose work in this world is nearing its end, even at a comparatively early physical age. Whereas Sophocles, for instance, did not write his farewell until he was ninety or so, when he wrote *Oedipus at Colonus*, Shakespeare died in 1616 when he was only fifty-two, and the date attributed to *The Tempest* is 1611. He therefore had about five years left in which we may imagine him living through the experience of old age foreshadowed in the epilogue and emerging perhaps into that state which Jung called, at the end of his life, kinship with all things and the eternal in man. Writing of *The Tempest* in a letter,[21] Charles Williams said that no poet would *decide* to give up writing poetry, but he felt that Shakespeare was saying "I will give up all imposition of views. Life shall be just life."

> . . . Please you draw near . . .
> Now my charms are all o'erthrown,
> And what strength I have's mine own—
> Which is most faint . . .

These lines express the inevitable experience which comes either gradually or suddenly with the loss of the fiery energy of spirit and body which has been ours, or so we have felt, in varying degrees and which has brought us success, power, a sense of achievement and of meaning in our chosen ways of life. Not only mystics, poets, and artists of all kinds, but many others may have been conscious throughout, as was Prospero, that his Ariel is not his own; but no one can live through the conflicts of a human life without having often identified his ego with the Ariel within or, at the other extreme, which is the dark side of the same thing, with Caliban and the sense of inferiority which besets all men and women when they believe that life and the sins of others have stolen their birthright and made them slaves to circumstance.

This loss may be experienced consciously or unconsciously in old age, and it brings with it, particularly perhaps for those who, like Prospero, have recognized the necessity of letting Ariel go at the right moment, the danger of despair. There are still a few simple and childlike men and women remaining in our world who do not encounter any such experience because, like primitives such as the Bushmen described by Laurens van der Post, they have not had to encounter consciously the split between conscious and unconscious. But the majority of civilized people have lost all sense of the original innocence, and, never having succeeded in releasing Ariel from the tree where he is imprisoned, have lived all their lives in a state of identification with ego consciousness and therefore of possession by unconscious motives. They may remain aware of underlying despair, but they are apt to sink into a querulous state as they lose their energies with age. This is often expressed by projecting all their ills onto circumstances and sometimes onto those on whom they now depend and most need. Since there is no separate identity there can be no relatedness, no exchange.

They may, as has been said, make pointless attempts to hold on to youthful activities or become more and more apathetic. Either way <u>they are held</u> by a spell in the prison of the ego, <u>alone on their "bare island."</u>

Our concern here is with the loss of energy, the seeming loss of that which has seemed most valuable in our souls, when all emotional experience of the numinous has faded. The more conscious man or woman will look open-eyed into the void, which is expressed by Shakespeare in those lines

> Now my charms are all o'erthrown,
> And what strength I have's mine own . . .

There is nothing left except the ego and the rapid decline of the ego's power to achieve, to do what it chooses, to work or play as before, to concentrate, to control. Every action required of either body or mind may indeed begin to feel like "a weight, heavy as frost and deep almost as life," as Charles Williams wrote, quoting Wordsworth, in a letter towards the end of his life.

In these later letters from which A. M. Hadfield has quoted in her book, *Charles Williams: An Exploration of His Life and Work*, Williams has defined this kind of experience as it came to him, with great beauty and clarity. He, like Shakespeare, was under sixty years old at the time. He tells how one feels forever thrust back to the beginning again—"elasticity and fire" have gone (Ariel indeed) and so in this blank one must know, he says, "something else"—"and not only something else but something almost of another kind."

It is this "something else" that Prospero must now seek. For him it will come through recognition of his need, his human need, for "the other"; he had lived all his life both before and after coming to the island in the study of the numinous powers in the unconscious to the exclusion of most of the simple exchanges of human relationships, and he had come to the state of treating all these powers as his own, until his hubris reached the point of claiming power not only over the elements but over death itself—

Graves at my command
Have waked their sleepers, oped, and let 'em forth
At my so potent art.

In Charles Williams's last book, *All Hallow's Eve,* he writes of the adept Simon, showing how this magician was brought finally through this same hubris to the beginnings of failure and how he descended then to lesser magical tricks which were his undoing. Williams remarks that one of the essential laws for any practitioner of magic is never to go back to such things once he has acquired greater powers. We may extend that thought to all our power-seeking work whether in the world or in our efforts to "improve" ourselves inwardly, seeking so-called spirituality. We cannot go back to dependence on techniques and attitudes that have been earlier an essential help on our journey.

This is reminiscent of Prospero's final tricks played on Caliban and his companions just before his awakening and his sacrifice—"But this rough magic I here abjure. . . . I'll break my staff. . . ." Whereas Simon is forever lost, Prospero is saved and the enormous difference between them is symbolized precisely by the difference in their treatment of their respective daughters, which is in fact the equivalent of what they are doing to their own souls. For Simon, his daughter, Betty, was brought into the world by him as a tool which he used ruthlessly to increase his powers and whom he intended to murder and, through her, extend his domination into the Beyond. For Miranda, Prospero retained a true and tender love, which, as we have seen, grew strong first through their sufferings on the lonely voyage to the island. Through this one human tie and selfless tenderness he was preserved from the final invasions by the destructive side of his great gifts of inner vision, and more especially by his sacrifice of possessiveness, his gift to her of freedom to love Ferdinand. In other words, he had always been moved in his inmost heart, no matter how arrogant and blind his ego might become, by love in its truest sense. "All shall be well and all manner of thing shall be well by the purification of the motive in the ground of our beseeching," to use the words of the Lady Julian of Norwich and T. S. Eliot in *The Four Quartets.*

All shall be well when we are free from the will to dominate people or things or our own souls. Our superficial motives cannot finally destroy us if we are aware of and attend to the point of real love in the ground of being—even if that attention be sadly weak and often forgotten. All the most lofty intentions are meaningless if at the root is a rejection of that love. Yet even in that hell of refusal "It," "He," "She" is there in the darkness, and there is much evidence which reinforces a belief that at the moment of death itself the root of love is suddenly revealed for who knows how many.

Simon speaks continually of "love" and "heals" many people, but he intends only power; and he is overwhelmed, annihilated by that very power he has invoked. Prospero boasts and talks about his wrongs and his prowess, but he has known love and seeks it in his "ground," and it breaks through into his whole life with his sacrifice of power and his recognition of "this thing of darkness" as his own.

Nevertheless, a lifetime of isolation from ordinary human meetings and conflicts has still to be paid for, before the old man can know freedom of spirit. Therefore in the epilogue we hear that strange appeal in which he expresses to all those others, to whom he has thought himself superior through his superhuman powers, his realization that he is dependent on them now as simple human beings. If they will respond to him as he now is in his weakness, then the spell that could keep him forever imprisoned in what he now recognizes as the sterility of his ego can be broken, and he can return to the world of humankind and so find his death in peace when the time is ripe. None of us can enter into human exchanges without response. There is profound wisdom underlying the words, "Now that I have . . . pardon'd the deceiver . . . release me from my bonds with the help of your good hands." For it is surely universally true that every free relationship or exchange of love is born only when there is forgiveness in the hearts of those involved. Prospero says he has pardoned "the deceiver"—he doesn't say anything of those onto whom he had projected his own deceits. We may therefore infer that, with Caliban, he has at last seen and forgiven the deceiver in himself who had come near to murdering him. "This thing of darkness I acknowledge mine."

> Gentle breath of yours my sails,
> Must fill, or else my project fails
> Which was to please. . . .

To me the hidden meaning of all this is that he has given up all his power to dominate but he retains in this powerless state his basic intention of affirming joy and beauty, however emotionally unfelt it may have become to his own ego; and to do this he needs response. He is at last in a state of forgiveness, and humble enough to know that without "the other" he might very easily succumb to the despair which would deny the very existence of "something else" beyond the "art to enchant"— that "something else" which Charles Williams knew as the end of his life approached. He affirmed this certainty in those later letters. The vital thing now, he said, was to affirm the "life of glory" which he knew to be present everywhere, at all times, however little he might emotionally feel it. He even said that it might seem to the liver of this life (meaning the ego) largely dull; but he knew himself at the last happily "superfluous" instead of miserably powerless.

So in the epilogue, Shakespeare goes on to define the only possible release from the disintegration and despair which threaten most powerfully those whose lives have been spent in the service of a creative spirit. Jung describes how such a "daemon" had driven him all his life at the expense of everything else. Every man and woman, even those who do not stand out as obvious "creators," must, like Prospero, come at last to the point of recognizing that this "spirit" which is alive in all humankind will not remain forever at the beck and call of his ego, giving him a sense of meaning and achievement in his life to the end. Ariel set free does not die, however little we may feel his presence; he becomes that "something else"—the spirit of joy beyond all the ego's desires and emotions. He is then not only daytime joy, he rides on the bat's back in the darkest of our nights—a flame of joy in the pain. Only if we pursue him still and will not let go does he turn to nightmare and despair.

As expressed in the writings or paintings or music or spoken words of the great ones and as experienced and lived silently by so many unknown and obscure, the "pattern of the glory" (as Charles Williams calls it) is not, as we have perhaps imagined, an apex of achievement, even in the inner world of the soul and the spirit. Rather is it known in the agonies and dangers of a gradual letting go, through which alone the emptiness comes, into which the glory may enter.

Jung, after describing a lifetime spent in the search for self-knowledge and the opening of doors in all he met to this essential quest for wholeness, wrote at the end of *Memories, Dreams, Reflections:*

The older I have become, the less I have understood or had insight into or known about myself. . . .

When Lao-tzu says: "All are clear, I alone am clouded," ✓ he is expressing what I now feel in advanced old age. Lao-tzu is the example of a man with superior insight who has seen and experienced worth and worthlessness and who at the end of his life desires to return into his own being, into the eternal unknowable meaning. The archetype of the old man who has seen enough is eternally true. At every level of intelligence this type appears, and its lineaments are always the same, whether it be an old peasant or a great philosopher like Lao-tzu. This is old age, and a limitation. Yet there is so much that fills me: plants, animals, clouds, day and night, and the eternal in man.[22]

This is the archetype of the old man who at the end faces the growing realization that he knows nothing. Then comes the moment when he either succumbs to the despair which threatened Prospero—or passes beyond all meaning *and* meaninglessness to that "something else" which is, in Jung's words, the eternal in man and kinship with all things. Shakespeare expresses the depths of Prospero's experience of this archetype of the old man in the last six lines of the epilogue.

And my ending is despair,
Unless I am relieve'd by prayer,
Which pierces so, that it assaults
Mercy itself, and frees all faults.
As you from crimes would pardon'd be
Let your indulgence set me free.

Prayer, Forgiveness, Exchange, Mercy, and Freedom—these five are brought together here, and if we penetrate to their meaning for every human being we find light in the darkness of increasing age.

prayer   Prayer, says Prospero, is the *way* to the Mercy, to Forgiveness, to Freedom. We cannot pass over this word, equating it superficially with its simple meaning of asking for something, longing for what we perceive to be the good, begging for a desired result—even when we sincerely add the easily spoken words "if it be thy will." The necessity, in Shakespeare's words, is the kind of prayer that *pierces* through to the Mercy, where the opposites unite in pardon—the kind of prayer that costs everything because it reaches beyond every demand for results. Meister Eckhart once said that we must let go even of the demand to know eternity and God.

Yet the word "prayer" continues to mean an "asking" even when it ceases to be an asking *for* anything at all. I think again of Eliot's phrase after quoting Dame Julian of Norwich: "All shall be well . . . by the purification of the motive in the ground of our beseeching." All prayer, whether spoken or silent, purified or not, proceeds quite simply and uninterruptedly from that which *moves* each one of us in the "ground" of our thinking, feeling, and actions—from the fundamental *motive* of our lives. It can be said that we all get what we basically desire—though very often not in the way that we have imagined it. Indeed it can manifest just as easily in experience of the polar opposite of our conscious desires, when we pursue these without any purification or motive. But, in some form or another, from the ground of our being and our beseeching we are choosing how our own fate will be experienced. We all have the opportunity to receive the gift of freedom and to mediate this freedom to others. It is this kind of freedom that Prospero speaks of in the epilogue.

There are many levels of "beseeching" and it is very difficult to know ourselves well enough so that we reach beyond all our various longings for ourselves or for others, beyond even the agonized and right human desire to save others from their suffering, or to be released from our own. Even Christ prayed to be spared, but it was not his fundamental desire. That was unshakably to accept the necessity of his unique destiny.

This is the nature of "intercession"—a beautiful word derived from the Latin *inter cedere*, meaning "to yield between"—and it is this kind of prayer of which Prospero is in need from those who have responded to his life story—the prayer of which we are all in need.

The crucifixion is the greatest of all images of this "yielding between," the total yielding of God himself between earth and heaven, nailed to the opposites. He carried the suffering and the sins of the world, as we in our small degree may carry for another when we are thus yielded; but Christ's at-one-ment did not mean that we were relieved of our own necessity to sin and to suffer. The incarnation of "cosmogonic love" gives to each the freedom to choose—that is to find his own truth or his own error and to live his choice to the end. We may remember here the two thieves on either side of Christ, crucified with him. Their sins were the same, their penalties the same; only their choices were different. One said "yes," the other "no," to the facts, to the Fact of Love between them. Every true "yielding between" in any man or woman is a prayer that pierces through to the Mercy, to the love which is the reality of the universe.

C. G. Jung used to tell his students that the worst thing an analyst could do for his patients was to try to take away their neurotic suffering on the surface, thereby perhaps stealing from them the one thing that could lead them to greater consciousness of the motives in their "ground." Those in the healing professions all too often do not understand this truth and on which levels it applies. The true healer is always an "intercessor," not a remover of symptoms, which then simply go from one part of the psyche to another. Interceding by his own experience of suffering, he carries for the other—as the other carries for him or another. Moreover the word to "intercede" is very near to the word to "forgive" or to "pardon." To "give for," to "yield between" in their true meanings are each an expression of the love which "endures all things, bears all things" without any demand.

In Charles Williams' *All Hallow's Eve*, which, as I have said earlier, was his last published book, there is a scene carrying images of this kind of intercession and the forgiveness from which it springs, that once it has been read—and both seen and heard in the imagination—expresses these things far better than any abstract words. Simon the Clerk, the magician, had come to his daughter as she slept, ready, he thought, to send her into death and beyond under the spell of his will. But Betty had just been in contact with her recently dead friend, Lester, who sought forgiveness for her indifference to Betty's sufferings in their earlier life. Their conversation together had passed briefly through an affirmation of mutual pardon to a state of love beyond it, and Lester was there when Simon came. There is no mention of the words "prayer" or "God" or "intercession"—but it simply *happens*, because Lester is at once aware that her friend is in some deep unknown trouble as she sleeps and, therefore, set free by forgiveness, Lester quite naturally is quite willing in her heart to do anything at all to help, whatever the need. She finds herself standing behind the sleeping girl at the head of the bed, unseen by Simon, and she then feels the impact of his magical powers, his incantation of murder without any idea of what it is that threatens. She receives it in place of her friend as it creeps up from her feet to destroy her soul. Betty is free, but Lester, though she feels herself lying back on a wooden support, is now in extreme danger—until the sleeping Betty calls her name "Lester" in her sleep. It is a symbolic affirmation of Lester's individual being by one who loves her—and that one human name spoken unconsciously in love breaks the terrible power of the evil in Simon, as he works through his incantation of the reversed name of God. The two girls were in no way trained to what is known as prayer, had no formal religious background to guide them. They simply forgave, and followed the wonder and love of their newly discovered friendship in the simplest possible "yielding" and "giving for" in the present moment. The motive in the depths of each one's being—one in this world, the other in the Beyond—was now rooted and grounded in love, and all their asking would henceforth pierce to the Mercy without thought of any specific outcome.

prayer

Recently I happened to read another quite startling image of this "piercing" prayer. It is in a poem by George Herbert (1593–1633) called "Prayer"—a poem which is simply a list of all the many images which for him symbolized the nature of prayer. One of them is "Christ-side-piercing-spear." Whatever, we ask, has prayer to do with the seemingly random hostile act of a soldier carrying out the crucifixion of felons, as he thought? There is a brief account in St. John's Gospel, but it was the beginning of legends which culminated in the myth of the Grail when this was linked with Christianity. The blood and water that, according to St. John, flowed from the wound made by the soldier's spear after Jesus was dead was caught in the cup, the Grail, and became the lifeblood, the water of life, the inner nourishment of all who sought its meaning. But how could such a momentary impulse by an indifferent "enemy" be called "prayer"? Rightly the legend of Longinus affirmed his awakening to truth after the act. Could it be that mankind's fundamental prayer for meaning will bring to each man and woman the answer hidden in the symbols of blood and water if only we are *there* with the empty cup of our lives to receive it—that is, attending to whatever the present moment may bring? Then perhaps from the least expected source, perhaps from a rejected and blind part of ourselves, the spear may suddenly pierce to the heart of love, when God has seemed wholly dead.

Prayer, then, is ultimately a state of being, not a specific intention, though our "intentions" on other levels are still valid and not to be forgotten. There are in all ages a very few who live their whole lives "yielded between" earth and heaven, humanity and God, and in the East it has always been held true that all of us depend on them for life in the real sense. For most of us, it is a matter of momentary glimpses in our meetings with each other, but it is on our recognition of our vital responsibility for awareness as individuals of this kind of prayer that so much depends for us all. Shakespeare's epilogue to *The Tempest* expresses with great simplicity and power one old man's breakthrough to his need for intercession, and for that which is implicit in the beautiful word "mercy," bringing the great themes of forgiveness and prayer together. Mercy is the compassion— the suffering *with* all creation and God, and it takes us beyond all need for specific pardon, "freeing all faults."

There is a wonderful moment in Robert Browning's *The Ring and the Book* when the dying Pompilia exclaims of her cruel husband who has tortured and murdered her, "I pardon him? . . . I am saved by him so as by fire. . . ." When the greatest wrongs that we have suffered, even our own worst faults, are known at last as indeed the saving grace, the refining fire of which T. S. Eliot writes in "Little Gidding," without which we could never find the restored life, then the thought of pardon or being pardoned has no more relevance. Then the exchanged life of each with each, of every individual with God, would be known as one with the Mercy which is the mystery of love. "He saved others; himself he could not save." It is as true of all of us as it was of Christ, although spoken by his enemies. It is vitally necessary to remind ourselves in this time of hyper-active longing to save others, that others are saved only by our bearing of our own necessity with the "*intention* of joy" (Charles Williams' phrase).

"Mercy"

The *American Heritage Dictionary* tells us that the oldest known root of the word "mercy" is probably the Etruscan *merc*, from which such words as commerce and merchant are derived. It is therefore connected with basic images of exchange—value given and received between people. Like so many other meanings hidden in our language, the word commerce, debased to commercialism, has lost much of its dignity, since it often signifies greed for money through dishonest efforts to destroy competitors. But the root meaning of exchange persisted and developed in another context, its meaning deepening through the French *merci* to grateful response and kindness of heart, and finally to the compassion and forgiveness, including all our share of darkness, whereby we are able to open ourselves to the Mercy. This is the ultimate "exchange" that, when we come to a final letting go, may reveal to us the whole.

merci

It is a lovely thing to connect the constantly used *merci*, meaning "thank you" in France, with the Mercy that frees all faults. It has become (like our own "good-bye," for instance: "God be with you"), a polite formula used without feeling or thought—but even when unconsciously spoken, words have power—and often it carries between people the courtesy that is a mark of the presence of love. One of the phrases occurring often in Julian of Norwich's book is "Our courteous Lord." It hits me every time with a rare delight. Jung expresses the same "courtesy" of the divine reality when, at the very end of that passage about the love on which we are all utterly dependent, he says that, with this dependence, we are also always given the freedom to *choose* between truth and error. This is God's courtesy; we may say "yes" to forgiveness and pierce to Mercy or say "no" and choose imprisonment in the past and future of the ego.

Mercy, says Prospero, when we pierce to its heart frees all faults; and now we come to the last two lines of all:

As you from crimes would pardon'd be
Let your indulgence set me free.

The old man knows, has now experienced to the full, what it means to set Ariel free, and what it costs to give it all to his enemies, and even to the despised Caliban, as well as to those he has loved—Miranda, Gonzalo, Ariel—the freedom to be themselves. He has let go of all thought of revenge or of changing other people for the better, even of changing himself. He is as he is—"Life is just life." But for him as for all of us there is a final need—the humility to know that our ultimate freedom from the "half-tied vision of things," as Merton called it, depends upon response from the "other"—from that other in those whose lives we have touched which will, beyond all projection, respond to that which we are and set us free with divine courtesy to live our necessity to the end.

These thoughts bring an awareness of how extremely difficult it is to set another wholly free—and, harder still, to let go of the chains we wind around ourselves. We can only approach it through a growing understanding of <u>what letting go really is</u>. To find it, our way lies paradoxically through the acceptance of fully responsible bonds and boundaries; for without these, love is merely the desire to possess, whether it is lustful or so-called spiritual. We have to experience bondage on many levels and with great suffering before we can begin to know the meaning of freedom. For freedom is not license to do what we want to do on any level, or to take what we imagine we need, however "good" in our eyes, condemning the ways of others. We are free only when our fundamental motives are transformed. Glibly we talk of "the free world" and omit to ask how free am I in my own inner world—and how free do I allow others to be. We may in some situations be called upon to stand up and fight those who "trespass" against us, but if we do it without forgiveness and therefore without compassion, we shall never be freed from our own trespassing, never know freedom of spirit.

It is wonderful to discover that <u>the root of the word "free" is "pri," meaning quite simply "love"</u>; "pri" is also the origin of our word "friend," of the name of the Nordic goddess of love, Frigg, and of her day, Friday—which has been for Christians through the centuries the day of the darkness, of the "nailing" in a total bondage, from which freedom is born.

Given that response from the "other"—the true self in those who are his "audience"—and as we respond with our own gratitude and joy to Shakespeare's vision, we may imagine Prospero standing there empty, forgiving and forgiven, and watch the shadow of despair move finally away from him as he knows himself free, as Ariel is free, "happily superfluous" now, and yet also a unique and essential part of the great web of exchange that is the universe of "cosmogonic love."

Shakespeare in his last years seems to have been moved to write again and again about the shining beauty of forgiveness after great wrongs, and rightly are these plays called Romances in the best sense of that word. All kinds of improbable things happen, but the inner truth that is Romance is as real as any prosaic fact, and can be met over and over again in our lives. Some words spoken by Cymbeline during the last scene in that play are a wonderful summing up of the joy that is spread by the free spirit, the free heart. He is describing his daughter, Imogen, who is perhaps the most truly whole—mature and wise yet childlike, humorous and warmhearted yet clearheaded—of all Shakespeare's splendid androgynous women. I quote Cymbeline here as a kind of epilogue to the words of Prospero in his epilogue.

> . . . see,
> Posthumus anchors upon Imogen;
> And she, like harmless lightning, throws her eye
> On him, her brothers, me, her master, hitting
> Each object with a joy: the counterchange
> Is severally in all.

Her freedom evokes joy and pardon in all the others *severally*—individually, not collectively—in the degree of their awareness. Having said this, Cymbeline leads their thoughts and ours to worship in the temple, just as Gonzalo, at the end of *The Tempest*, lifts our eyes to the gods, in recognition of the unknown origin, source and end, in which we "live and move and have our being." "Here," he says, "in a poor isle all of us have found ourselves where no man was his own."

LITTLE GIDDING

AS I WROTE OF the piercing through to the Mercy for which Prospero waited after freeing Ariel, I remembered a woman's dream which I heard some four or five years ago. In it the dreamer was looking at one page of a huge calendar divided into squares. She wondered whether each square represented a day, a week, a month, or a year of life. Her gaze was fixed on the last line and a half of squares, in each of which were written the words "Of the Mercy"—ten of them, perhaps, in all. The squares above these—many, reaching up beyond her sight— had, she thought, varying notations in them, but she ignored these in the dream, her attention concentrated in awe on those final squares; and she thought with hope that at the end of her life she might possibly come to know—even if only for a few hours or days or minutes—the emptiness that is the Mercy, the Compassion, which contains all opposites. At the time of hearing the dream I myself had little experience of the *kind* of darkness, the long-drawn-out "letting go" through which, I am now certain, a man or woman approaches the "piercing" prayer that may ultimately break through to the Mercy.

The use of the preposition "of" in the dream is a matter for reflection. We might expect rather "In the Mercy," pointing to the absorption of the ego into the Self, or simply "the Mercy," leading us to think of mercy as the last hope of a dying person. The word "of" is more subtle. If we look up that preposition in the dictionary we see at once how enormously varied are its uses and that they include diametrically opposite meanings varying with the words and images used before the "of." It may indicate, for instance, either a close bond or a separation, closeness, or distance. One may be a friend of or an enemy of the Mercy. Those last squares of a life in the dream perhaps mean that finally the Mercy becomes the only reality in any life, but that the individual remains free to choose whether he or she will let go of everything else so that the new man who is the creation of the Mercy will be born, or whether he will hold on to the old man, to rejection of that emptiness which is the fullness of the Mercy.

I have quoted already from three or four of those who in this twentieth century have written about their experiences towards the end of their lives—a poet-novelist, a psychologist, a monk (Charles Williams, C. G. Jung, Thomas Merton). There is, however, a passage in another poet's work, in T. S. Eliot's "Little Gidding," the last of the *Four Quartets*, in which he defines, in words that pierce to the heart of the darkness of aging, the kind of experiences out of which the purging fire may bring us to the forgiveness, the Mercy, the "acausal orderedness" (Jung's phrase) of the dance of creation. At this point I urge any reader to read the poem itself, especially the lines beginning "Knowing myself yet being someone other" and ending "Where you must move in measure like a dancer." In writing of the impact on oneself of a poem, one may easily destroy the beauty of the poetry for others, unless it has first been read with fresh and open mind and heart for itself alone.

The poet had met, as he walked in the grey dawn, a stranger in whom he recognized a composite image of all the "masters" and teachers of his past life. This would include, especially for one who has known inner "gurus" and guides, all those influences arising from the search for wisdom which have determined the direction and inspired the enthusiasms of an individual life. The meeting takes place at that point of inter-section, as Eliot calls it, of time and space with eternity. The stranger speaks and urges him to let go finally of all the thoughts and theories he has been taught in the past, and of his own as well, for such things have served their purpose and he must await a new "language" for the time ahead. He asks for forgive-ness for both the bad *and the good* in his teaching, and tells his old pupil that he too needs forgiveness from those he has taught.

This brings a memory of Prospero's drowning of his book, an essential element in his transformation before he too could for-give and be forgiven. The whole passage carries an echo of Shakespeare's epilogue to *The Tempest*. It also brings back the words of Eliot's contemporary, Charles Williams, which I have already quoted, of how the loss of old ways of thought and feel-ing brought to him a sense of making room for "something else," "something almost of another kind"—surely Eliot's

"new language." I imagine it as the language beyond all definition in words, beyond all definition in words, beyond cause and
effect—a language that has been heard for thousands of years
by the sages.

The "someone other" in the poet, however, has more to say
to him of the experiences through which his ego must pass
before he can hear that "other voice"—that "something else."
He says he will disclose "the gifts reserved for age"—the gifts
that will crown his entire life. It is hard indeed as we reflect on
the lines that follow to remember that these things are blessed
gifts—gifts to be accepted in thankfulness if we are to fulfill
the meaning of our lives.

The gifts are three. First, the changes taking place in the
body—for some a sudden change and loss of physical health, or
a gradual lessening of the energies which have flowed through
the senses. Sight may grow dim, or hearing less acute; taste,
smell, and touch may lose their power to delight us. Many
activities on which we have depended become impossible.
Such losses may deprive us of much of the "enchantment"
which we have taken for granted as a channel of meaning. The
poet stresses this loss of enchantment and hints at the danger
of the fall into despair, of which Prospero also spoke even
when the old man had at last willingly consented to let go of
his enchanting and enchanted world. The fruits of a long life
may at this point seem indeed bitter, carrying no promise for
the future but a prospect of slowly increasing loss of energy.
The ego in fact always depends for its supremacy in the psyche

on fantasies of future achievement of pleasure. The Self lives only in the present moment. For a creative person this loss of perception through the senses may be an even greater threat, a separation between body and soul that strips meaning from both.

The second gift, says Eliot, is helpless rage at the terrifying folly of men and of their laughter at things which are not, we discover, even faintly amusing, but tragically serious. We cry out in frustrated horror at the blindness of those in political power; we see behind the exuberance of youth the shadow of violence or the excesses into which so many fall, and behind the beauty of romantic love the seeds of jealousy, possessiveness, and hate; and we shrink at the laughter which is the joy of life, subtly decaying into the laughs that wound and pierce the dignity of man or woman. And so we may end through this rage identified with all that we rage against. This is a truth that becomes daily more evident as we watch the increasing intolerance of many who fight for good causes. "How with this rage shall beauty hold a plea whose action is no stronger than a flower?[23]—a question to which Shakespeare's gifts to us of poetry are the answer. Only the creative imagination in each of us finds the place beyond rage, which is truly compassion and the laughter of joy.

Third and last is the gift of memories, which, in the old, grow stronger and more vivid as they look back over the stories of their lives. If we are able to look at the past clear-eyed, we shall recognize how many of our acts and achievements which we thought virtuous, kind, and good, were also the cause of much harm to others. If we have achieved praise and recognition we experience moments of horror at what appears now as the hypocrisy of the ego always at bottom concerned with its own merit and comfort, and most dangerously of all, its own spiritual merit.

Jung wrote towards the end of his life (in *The Undiscovered Self*) of the inevitable dark side of all "good" words which, while bringing healing perhaps or relief of suffering, will at the same time contribute to a loss of "health" or well-being in another context. There is only one answer to this law of the world of cause and effect; it lies in the individuals who, passing through and integrating the opposites in themselves, enter the measure of the dance in all creation. We all do as much harm as good except in those rare moments when we are aware of the dance in which the darkness is an essential part of the healing which is wholeness. Nevertheless, on that level of cause and effect we each must still fulfill our work in the world and commit ourselves to "the good" as we perceive it, while at the same time never losing sight of the truth that wholeness is born of the acceptance of the conflict of human and divine in the individual psyche.

Thus Eliot affirms that these exceedingly painful memories are gifts which may bring us to the crown of life. The loss of energy and of enchantment, the rage of projection of our hidden darkness onto others, or onto circumstances, the suffering hidden in our memories—all these, once they are accepted, become the essentials of liberation; and the love is born that frees us at last from both future and past—from the identification of Self with ego. Eliot's image of that freedom is the measure of the dance into which we may enter if we have passed through the "refining fire," the purging flame of integration of these strange gifts. Shakespeare's word for this dance, in Prospero's epilogue, as also the word in the modern dream quoted above, is Mercy— and the Buddhist equivalent is Compassion, the Christian *Agape*. Among the images, that of the dance is perhaps the most powerful of all, especially in this time of the discoveries about the nature of the subatomic world, which point to the final unity of matter and spirit, of time and the timeless, of the dancer and the dance. Mystics and great artists have always experienced this, and in all primitive societies it was unconsciously expressed in the measure of their dances. Moreover, there is no dance without individual dancers; and no dancer without the dance. Subjective and objective are one as we "move in measure like a dancer" in the "acausal order" of creator and created. Thus, through memories re-experienced as story, the life of the individual begins to move in a circle around the still point of the Center. It is no longer the straight line from birth to death emerging from darkness and disappearing into darkness again. It is a small pattern, unique and constant, in the dance of creation. There is a footnote in Jorge Luis Borges' essay, "The Mirror of Enigmas," in which he writes: "The steps a man takes from the day of his birth to the day of his death trace in time an inconceivable figure. The Divine Mind intuitively grasps that form immediately as men do a triangle. This figure (perhaps) has its given function in the economy of the universe."[24]

These gifts reserved for age, as described in a few lines of great poetry, are not, as I said when writing of *The Tempest*, confined to those who live very long lives physically. They may come to anyone who has lived his life to the full and is aging—growing—in a true sense; nor do they come suddenly but recur with deepening intensity for a longer or shorter time. In the undifferentiated unconscious every image flows into every other and *is* every other. But woman and then man, having eaten the apple and chosen to know good and evil, must leave Eden, the infantile Paradise, and go individually on the long journey in the dimension of time in which each may learn through the bitter conflicts of the opposites to discriminate every smallest thing or image as unique and separate. Thus we gradually approach the "objective cognition" which Jung called the central secret and find at last that, having distinguished the ego from the Self which is ours and not ours, we begin to enter the dance: and now there comes a change—it may even be felt as a complete reversal.

As I wrote the above paragraph, I was delighted when a memory from Lewis Carroll's *Alice in Wonderland* drifted up in my mind.

> *"You are old, Father William," the young man said,*
> *"And your hair has become very white;*
> *And yet you incessantly stand on your head—*
> *Do you think, at your age, it is right?"*
>
> *"In my youth," Father William replied to his son,*
> *"I feared it might injure the brain;*
> *But now that I'm perfectly sure I have none,*
> *Why, I do it again and again."*

I have sometimes thought that each stage of the letting go of an old conceptual approach to the meaning of life, on which we have so far depended for our inner journey, is like having to stand on one's head; but if, like Father William, we finally realize that the human brain cannot bring enlightenment, and that our much prized reasoning, though an essential of the way, answers none of our ultimate questions, we then perhaps as happily stand on our heads as on our feet!

It is time to let go of dependence on those splendid methods, unquestioned techniques perhaps, and the collectively sanctioned beliefs of centuries. The task for many years has been rightly centered on the differentiation of our own unique being as an individual from its unconscious subjective confusion. We seek to make conscious, slowly and painfully, all the images that come to us, that have influenced us since birth, through our parents and ancestors, through our environment and schooling, through our cultural and national attitudes and traditions, asking again and again the basic question, "Who am I?" We have truly come to some degree of objectivity about the ego, and our projections become more and more easily recognizable. We glimpse the possibility of that new life in which the briefest meetings with others can be "immediate presence"— in which love flows clear-eyed into all our exchanges and without the involuntary emotion which is both possessive and possessed. There is then no need to regress to unconscious mixing, for we are the other and yet not the other—one yet many. It is now, after the long process of analytical separation, that we suddenly feel the touch of that "new language" and of that "something almost of another kind." But between the old language and the new there must come the shock of awareness in which man experiences the truth that we know nothing about who we are and never shall. To quote again Jung's words, "The older I have become the less I have understood or had insight into or known about myself."[25]

To our wonder, we may find that now it is time to become aware of our oneness with everything and everyone other. Instead of "I am not this, I am not that person or thing or image," we begin to affirm, "I am both this and that" and to glimpse the meaning of "I am" as the name of God. This is in no way an *enantiodromia*, a reversal, objectivity becoming sub-jectivity again. It is rather the faint dawning of the awareness of the unity between these seemingly opposed attitudes to life. Now we may begin to hear that new language which is more in the nature of spontaneous song, the "music of God" in every happening, whether of pain or joy. The music is unique in you and in me and in every detail of the incarnate world, but how-ever simple or complex, however loud or soft, it will harmonize with the great "unstruck sound" of the totality. Dante in *The Paradiso* writes of the sound of the angels in the white rose as the humming of bees. It sounds through the entire universe. When we begin to hear it we approach the Mercy, and may sing with Angelus Silesius, "The rose has no why, it flowers because it flowers."

I return here to Prospero and his freeing of Ariel. It seemed to him that he had lost forever that which had brought "enchantment" to his spirit and meaning to his life. The

emptiness that followed brought him near to despair, and so it
must be for all seekers.

We may now look again at the fundamental meaning of the
word "enchantment." The word means a state of being
intensely filled with "chant," that is, with song (the *en-* here
indicates intensity). The secondary meaning of "to enchant"
(or to be enchanted) does specifically indicate a spell deliber-
ately put upon another, or the state of possession by such a
spell. The traditional magic spells were cast by the repetition
of words of power. In our time, this magic reaches our unconscious through repetitions of the media, proclaiming half-
truths. Prospero consciously renounced any *use* of the magic of
Ariel, as Odysseus let go of his drive to achievement, and they
were at once freed from the ego's manipulations and from the
dangers of possession. So they and every man or woman after
the inevitable time in the desert, when their "oars" were
planted in the earth and their sacrifices made, may surely hear
again in freedom the voice of Ariel from the "cowslip's bell"
and the "bat's back." We may then know the enchantment
beyond all binding in the music of which Yeats wrote these
beautiful lines in the latter part of his life:

> *An aged man is but a paltry thing,*
> *A tattered coat upon a stick, unless*
> *Soul clap its hands and sing, and louder sing*
> *For every tatter in its mortal dress,*
> *Nor is there singing school but studying*
> *Monuments of its own magnificence;*

> *And therefore I have sailed the seas and come*
> *To the holy city of Byzantium.*
>
> *O sages standing in God's holy fire*
> *As in the gold mosaic of a wall,*
> *Come from a holy fire, perne in a gyre*
> *And be the singing-masters of my soul.*[26]

Another poet of the twentieth century wrote not long before he died:

> *And if, in the changing phases of man's life*
> *I fall in sickness and in misery*
> *my wrists seem broken and my heart seems dead*
> *and strength is gone, and my life*
> *is only the leavings of a life:*
>
> *and still, among it all, snatches of lovely oblivion and snatches of*
>   *renewal*
> *odd, wintry flowers upon the withered stem, yet new, strange flowers*
> *such as my life has not brought forth before, new blossoms of me—*
>
> *then I must know that still*
> *I am in the hands of the unknown God,*
> *he is breaking me down to his new oblivion*
> *to send me forth on a new morning, a new man.*[27]

Thus the poets speak to us out of the darkness and danger of this age of transition in the dimension of time, that we may come at last to "move in measure like a dancer" in the midst of the "refining fire" and emerge singing in the joy which comes only when we no longer seek happiness. Then in the "hands of the unknown God" we may waken to "the new morning" where "the fire and the rose are one."

I end with these timeless words from an American Indian "Nightway" chant:

In old age wandering on a trail of beauty lively may I walk.
In old age wandering on a trail of beauty living again may I walk.
It is finished in beauty.

SUFFERING

"S<small>UFFERING</small>" <small>IS A WORD</small> used to express so many kinds of experience that its precision of meaning has been lost. The Latin verb *ferre* means "to bear," "to carry," and "suffer" derives from it, with the prefix "sub" meaning "under." This is reminiscent of the term "undercarriage"—that which bears the weight of a vehicle above the wheels—which is an apt image of the meaning of suffering in human life.

In contrast to the word "suffer," such terms as "affliction," "grief," and "depression" all bring images of weight bearing *down*. To be afflicted is to be struck down by a blow (*fligere:* to strike). "Grief" is derived from *gravare*, and to be depressed is to be pressed down. Only when we suffer in the full sense of the word do we *carry* the weight. A man may say, "I am so terribly depressed, I can't bear the suffering," when in fact he may not be suffering at all, but simply lying down under the weight of outer circumstances or inner mood.

There are, then, two kinds of experiences which we call suffering—that which is totally unproductive, the neurotic state

of meaningless depression, and that which is the essential condition of every step on the way to what C. G. Jung has called
individuation. Perhaps these images of weight under which we
fall and lie in self-pity, or of weight which we carry in full consciousness, may be a guideline in moments of darkness. The
blows of great affliction or grief are comparatively rare, but day-
to-day onslaughts of hurt feelings, black moods, exhaustion,
resentment, and, most deadly of all, false guilt, are the training
ground, and nothing is too small to offer us an opportunity to
choose between suffering and depression.

Deeply ingrained in the infantile psyche is the conscious or
unconscious assumption that the cure for depression is to
replace it with pleasant, happy feelings, whereas the only valid
cure for any kind of depression lies in the acceptance of real
suffering. To climb out of it any other way is simply a palliative,
laying the foundations for the next depression. Nothing whatever has happened to the soul. The roots of all our neuroses lie
here, in the conflict between the longing for growth and freedom and our incapacity or refusal to pay the price in suffering
of the kind which challenges the supremacy of the ego's
demands. This is the crux of the matter (and we may pause
here to recognize the exact meaning of the word "crux"). The
ego will endure the worst agonies of neurotic misery rather
than one moment of consent to the death of even a small part
of its demand or its sense of importance.

On humility

We can do something towards tracking down some of the
continual evasions of the ego by uncovering our fear of humiliation. From this fear of degradation in our own eyes or in the

eyes of others, real or imagined, comes a dead weight of moods and depression. For the truly humble person no humiliation exists. It is impossible to humiliate him or for him to feel humiliation, for "grades" and prestige, questions of his own merit or demerit, have no more meaning for him. But the way to humility lies through the pain of accepted humiliation. In the moment of picking it up and carrying it without any movement towards self-justification, we cease to be humiliated and begin to suffer. In this context, it is well to realize the extent to which we are all open in the unconscious to the present collective worship of what we may call "grades."

Worship is not too strong a word. The more the conscious ideal of the equality of man is proclaimed on the wrong levels, the more desperate becomes the unconscious urge to assert the difference, and the yearning for prestige of all kinds breaks loose from the natural hierarchies of being into the struggles of the ego for ascendancy. The inequalities of class in the aristocratic age, absurd though we may call them, were certainly less conducive to neurosis than the gradings of money, academic prowess, IQ's, and A's, B's, and C's in every department of life, which can so dominate our personal unconscious that we are busy grading our weaknesses day in and day out—a very different thing from searching them out and carrying them. The poison of false values thus invades every corner of the psyche. A question to be constantly asked in moods of weakness and depression is, "Am I grading myself or am I recognizing the golden opportunity to suffer and so to deny to some small degree the ego's demands for prestige?"

The worst stumbling block of all derives from this grading. There was no guilt involved in being born into this or that social class, but nowadays we are beset on every side by a false guilt which is inverted pride. If we do not rate a B or at least a C in every department of life, then we deem ourselves guilty. The puritanical strain in our heritage reinforces this until we can even allow our work on our inner life to engender a false sense of guilt about our physical, as well as our emotional, weaknesses.

Of course on one level it is true that any kind of symptom, physical or psychological, is a clue to the working of the unconscious which should be followed up at the right time. But, if we feel this deadly kind of guilt, it simply means that we cannot accept our human condition, that we have given way to hubris and are saying unconsciously, "I ought to be like God, free of all weakness," forgetting what happened to God Himself on the cross. The clues are to be worked upon, but the symptom itself is something to be wholly and freely accepted without egotistic guilt or any *demand* to be freed from it.

Hope for release is another thing, both natural and right, as also are the exterior efforts to come out of the sickness or mood. We are not excused from ordinary common sense by the fact that we accept the suffering and demand no release. In fact the two attitudes are one, and real acceptance will lead us to seek the appropriate help, whether medical skill in illness, the support of friends in grief, rest in exhaustion, work either physical or psychological in depression. Thus, we begin to build the "undercarriage" of suffering upon which the superstructure of our lives may securely rest and under which the wheels may move freely over the earth. The four-wheeled chariot is an ancient symbol of the Incarnation, and the thought of suffering as the undercarriage fits perfectly into this image. Suffering is that which carries the weight of the vehicle, distributing it over the fourfold wheels so that the driver may stand in safety and move towards his chosen goal.

However great our efforts may be to achieve this conscious attitude to suffering, we cannot succeed without an awareness that, in spite of apparent senselessness, there is always an implicit universal meaning even in the carrying of small miseries. Every time a person exchanges neurotic depression for real suffering, he or she is sharing to some small degree in the carrying of the suffering of mankind, in bearing a tiny part of the darkness of the world. Such a one is released from his small personal concern into a sense of *meaning*. One may not be consciously thinking in those terms, but the transition can immediately be recognized by the disappearance of the frustrated pointlessness of mood and depression. It is as though we become aware of a new dimension. Meaning has entered the experience.

We may be emotionally moved and filled with horror and pity when we hear of the tragedies of human lives at a distance, but the emotions lift no burden, they carry nothing. In contrast, the smallest consent to the fierce, sharp pain of objective suffering in the most trivial-seeming matter may have an influence, as the Chinese sage puts it, "at a distance of a thousand miles." We may be entirely certain that some burden somewhere is lightened by our effort. Close at hand the effects are immediately visible. Those around us may know nothing of what is happening, but a weight is lifted from the atmosphere, or someone we love is set free to be himself, and the sufferer acquires a new clarity of vision and sensitivity to another's need. Nothing is as blinding as neurotic self-pity. We walk around in a fog.

There is a familiar example of the difference between objective suffering and subjective emotional reaction in its effect on others, which many people have experienced at some time in their lives if they have been seriously ill. A nurse, or anyone else who is close to another's pain, physical or psychic, if she reacts with intense personal emotion to the patient's misery, will either repress what she cannot bear and become hard and unfeeling, or else will increase the sick one's burden through her unconscious identification. A true nurse, by contrast, is always deeply concerned; she is compassionate (which means objectively "suffering with") but not invaded by emotional reactions. She is herself changed by the experience through the love that lives beyond emotion. The patient can literally be saved by this kind of "carrying" by another, but can be swamped and pushed deeper into misery by the unconscious reactions of those around him or her, however well they may be disguised. The difference is subtle but absolutely distinct when experienced.

Just as there is no cure for an inferior kind of love except a greater and more conscious love, so there is no cure for inferior so-called suffering except a greater kind of suffering. It is possible by intense conscious attention to pass through this door into the fiercer suffering which is linked to the whole, and then a strange thing may happen. We have lifted the weight and, instead of being crushed by it, we find it is extraordinarily light—"My yoke is easy, my burden is light." The pain remains but it is more like the piercing of a sword than a weight. "A sword shall pierce through thy own soul also, that the thoughts of many hearts may be revealed."[28] These are the prophetic words of the wise old man Simeon, spoken to Mary when she took her newborn child to the temple. We have shed blood, the sacrificial blood, and so we can experience joy, not just pleasant feelings and escape.

There is in man a fear of joy as keen as the fear of suffering pain, because true joy precludes the pleasant feeling of self-importance just as suffering precludes all the comforts of self-pity. No man can know the one without the other. It is important here to discriminate between the spurious joy of the martyr complex and the joy which is on the other side of the cross. Christ was not a martyr, going singing to his death. If we catch ourselves feeling noble on account of our sufferings, we may be perfectly sure that we are simply at the old trick of climbing out of depression into pleasant feeling—all the more dangerous because it is camouflaged as noble.

Real suffering belongs to innocence, not guilt. As long as we feel misery because we are full of remorse and guilt or shame over our weakness, all we experience is a loss of vital energy and no transformation takes place. But the minute we accept objectively the guilt and shame, the *innocent* part of us begins to suffer, the weight becomes a sword. We bleed, and the energy flows back into us on a deeper and more conscious level. This is real repentance as opposed to ego-centered shame, for it involves the recognition of the true guilt which lies always in our evasions of objective awareness.

For Christians, it is easy to give lip service to the "innocent victim," to Christ carrying in innocence the sin and suffering of the world. But rarely do we even think of the essential practical application of this truth in the smallest of our pains. Only when the *innocent* part of us begins to suffer is there life and creation within and around us; but for the most part, we prefer to remain caught in the vicious and totally unproductive circle of remorse and superficial complacency, followed by a repetition of the sin, more remorse, and so on. In the Book of Job, God's condemnation falls on the complacent rationality of the false comforters who assure Job that he could not possibly be suffering unless he were morally guilty. To Job, suffering but innocent, God's answer is simply to reveal Himself in His infinite power and glory, beyond rational explanation.

In these days when the media bring to us daily the sight and sound of the appalling sufferings of the innocent, we all have great need of reminders of the only way in which we can contribute to the healing of the terrible split between curse and blessing in our time.

The poets and great storytellers of all ages come to our aid. When one man takes up responsibility for his blindness without any false guilt, even in the smallest things, the self-pity and the projections of blame onto others or onto God drop away, and the blessing beyond the opposites is strengthened in our environment. It seems infinitesimal, but in Jung's words it may be the "make-weight that tips the scales." Thus we suffer the sword of objectivity, refusing nothing, so that the healing may reach "the hearts of many" without our conscious intention. It happens not through our willed efforts to improve the world, fine and right though these may be on another level, but to the degree to which the curse and the blessing have been experienced consciously as one in the psyche of the individual. It is an experience which as C. G. Jung wrote in *Mysterium Conjunctionis* reaches "the individual in stillness—the individual who constitutes the meaning of the world."

We began by defining a word. We end with another—the word "passion." Derived from the Latin *passio*, meaning suffering, it is used to define the sufferings of Christ. Commonly the word applies to any emotion which goes beyond the bounds of reason, consuming and possessing a man so that he is in a state of "enthusiasm," which, in its original meaning, is the state of being filled with the god, whether the god of anger, of love, or of hate.

When suffering breaks through the small personal context and exposes a man to the pain and darkness of life itself, the way is opened to that ultimate state of passion beyond all the passions of desire. There, being completely empty, as Christ was empty when He cried, "My God, my God, why hast Thou forsaken me?" he may finally come to be filled with the wholeness of God Himself.

NOTES

THE ODYSSEY

1. *The Odyssey*, E. V. Rieu translation, Penguin Classics.
2. Ibid.
3. *The Odyssey*, Robert Fitzgerald translation, Noonday Press.
4. T. S. Eliot, *The Four Quartets*.
5. For this insight into Dante's own probable temptation I am indebted to Jorge Luis Borges' essay on *The Divine Comedy* in his book *Labyrinths*. New York: New Directions, p. 212.
6. *The Odyssey*, Book Nine, Robert Fitzgerald translation.

KING LEAR

7. William Shakespeare, Sonnet 65.

THE TEMPEST

8. Charles Williams, *He Came Down from Heaven*.
9. See Oxynhyinthus Papyrus, Gospel of the Hebrews, quoted by Clement of Alexandria, text restored by E. White, in *The Apocryphal New Testament*, ed. M. R. James, 1927: "And ye shall know yourselves that ye are in God and God in you. And ye are the City of God."
10. *A Midsummer Night's Dream*, act 5, scene 1.
11. Ibid.
12. Clement of Alexandria (see note 9) speaks of a book called *Traditions of Matthias:* "The beginning of truth is to wonder at things, as Plato says in the Theatus, as Matthias in the Traditions, advising us: Wonder at things that are before thee, making this the first step to further knowledge."
13. Thomas Merton, *Asian Journal.* New York: New Directions, 1975, p. 233.
14. Charles Williams once commented on this breaking of Prospero's staff, saying, "Is this 'I'll give up writing'? Could any poet say so . . .

133

mightn't it rather mean, 'I'll break all imposition of views—life shall be just life'?"

15. *The Tempest*, act 3, scene 2.
16. *The Tempest*, stage directions, act 4, scene 1.
17. Laurens van der Post, *Yet Being Someone Other.* New York: William Morrow, 1982, p. 73.
18. Julian of Norwich, *Revelations on Divine Love,* ed. from the mss by Dom Roger Hudleston, O.S.B. Westminster, MD: Newman Press, 1952, 2d ed.
19. Liturgy for Easter Saturday.
20. C. G. Jung, *Memories, Dreams, Reflections.* New York: Pantheon, 1963, p. 358.
21. A. M. Hadfield, *Charles Williams: An Exploration of His Life and Work.* New York: Oxford University Press, 1983.
22. Jung, *Memories, Dreams, Reflections*, pp. 358–59.

LITTLE GIDDING

23. William Shakespeare, Sonnet 65.
24. Borges, *Labyrinths*, p. 212.
25. Jung, *Memories, Dreams, Reflections*, p. 358. See also my essay on *The Tempest*, p. 80.
26. W. B. Yeats, "Sailing to Byzantium."
27. D. H. Lawrence, "Shadows," in *The Complete Poems of D. H. Lawrence*, ed. Vivian de Sola Pinto and Warren Roberts, vol. 2. New York: Viking Press, pp. 226–27.

SUFFERING

28. Luke 2:35.

ABOUT THE AUTHOR

Helen M. Luke was born in 1904 in England. She received a master's degree in French and Italian literature from Somerville College, Oxford. Twenty years later she became interested in the work of C. G. Jung and studied at the Jung Institute in Zurich. After moving to the United States in 1949, she established an analytical practice in Los Angeles, then in 1962 founded the Apple Farm Community in Three Rivers, Michigan: "A center for people seeking to discover and appropriate the transforming power of symbols in their lives." She died in 1995 at Apple Farm.

OTHER BELL TOWER BOOKS

Books that nourish the soul, illuminate the mind,
and speak directly to the heart

Rob Baker
PLANNING MEMORIAL CELEBRATIONS
A Sourcebook
A one-stop handbook for a situation more and more of us
are facing as we grow older.
0-609-80404-9 Softcover

Thomas Berry
THE GREAT WORK
Our Way into the Future
The grandfather of Deep Ecology teaches us how to move
from a human-centered view of the world to one
focused on the earth and all its inhabitants.
0-609-60525-9 Hardcover
0-609-80499-5 Softcover

Cynthia Bourgeault
LOVE IS STRONGER THAN DEATH
The Mystical Union of Two Souls
Both the story of the incandescent love between two hermits
and a guidebook for those called to this path of soulwork.
0-609-60473-2 Hardcover

Madeline Bruser
THE ART OF PRACTICING
Making Music from the Heart
A classic work on how to practice music which combines
meditative principles with information on body
mechanics and medicine.
0-609-80177-5 Softcover

Marc David
NOURISHING WISDOM
A Mind/Body Approach to Nutrition and Well-Being
A book that advocates awareness in eating.
0-517-88129-2 Softcover

Joan Furman, MSN, RN, and David McNabb
THE DYING TIME
Practical Wisdom for the Dying and Their Caregivers
A comprehensive guide, filled with physical, emotional,
and spiritual advice.
0-609-80003-5 Softcover

Bernie Glassman
BEARING WITNESS
A Zen Master's Lessons in Making Peace
How Glassman started the Zen Peacemaker Order and
what each of us can do to make peace in our hearts
and in the world.
0-609-60061-3 Hardcover   0-609-80391-3 Softcover

Bernard Glassman and Rick Fields
INSTRUCTIONS TO THE COOK
A Zen Master's Lessons in Living a Life That Matters
A distillation of Zen wisdom that can be used equally well as
a manual on business or spiritual practice, cooking or life.
0-517-88829-7 Softcover

Niles Elliot Goldstein
GOD AT THE EDGE
*Searching for the Divine in Uncomfortable
and Unexpected Places*
A book about adventure, raw experience,
and facing inner demons.
Hardcover 0-609-60499-6

Greg Johanson and Ron Kurtz
GRACE UNFOLDING
Psychotherapy in the Spirit of the Tao-te ching
The interaction of client and therapist illuminated through
the gentle power and wisdom of Lao-tzu's ancient classic.
0-517-88130-6 Softcover

Selected by Marcia and Jack Kelly
ONE HUNDRED GRACES
Mealtime Blessings
A collection of graces from many traditions, inscribed in
calligraphy reminiscent of the manuscripts of medieval Europe.
0-609-80093-0 Softcover

Jack and Marcia Kelly

SANCTUARIES

A Guide to Lodgings in Monasteries, Abbeys, and Retreats of the United States

For those in search of renewal and a little peace; described by the *New York Times* as "the *Michelin Guide* of the retreat set."

0-517-88517-4 Softcover

Lorraine Kisly, ed.

✓ **ORDINARY GRACES**

Christian Teachings on the Interior Life

An essential collection of the deepest spiritual, religious, and psychological teachings of Christianity.

0-609-60674-3 Hardcover

Barbara Lachman

THE JOURNAL OF HILDEGARD OF BINGEN

A year in the life of the twelfth-century German saint— the diary she never had the time to write herself.

0-517-88390-2 Softcover

Stephen Levine

A YEAR TO LIVE

How to Live This Year as if It Were Your Last

Using the consciousness of our mortality to enter into a new and vibrant relationship with life.

0-609-80194-5 Softcover

Gunilla Norris
BEING HOME
A Book of Meditations
An exquisite modern book of hours,
a celebration of mindfulness in everyday activities.
0-517-58159-0 Hardcover

Marcia Prager
THE PATH OF BLESSING
Experiencing the Energy and Abundance of the Divine
How to use the traditional Jewish practice of calling down a
blessing on each action as a profound path of spiritual growth.
0-517-70363-7 Hardcover   0-609-80393-X Softcover

Saki Santorelli
HEAL THY SELF
Lessons on Mindfulness in Medicine
An invitation to patients and health care professionals to bring
mindfulness into the crucible of the healing relationship.
0-609-60385-X Hardcover   0-609-80504-5 Softcover

Rabbi Rami M. Shapiro
MINYAN
Ten Principles for Living a Life of Integrity
A primer for those interested to know
what Judaism has to offer the spiritually hungry.
0-609-80055-8 Softcover

Rabbi Rami M. Shapiro
WISDOM OF THE JEWISH SAGES
A Modern Reading of Pirke Avot
A third-century treasury of maxims on justice,
integrity, and virtue—Judaism's principal
ethical scripture.
0-517-79966-9 Hardcover

Jean Smith
THE BEGINNER'S GUIDE TO ZEN BUDDHISM
A comprehensive and easily accessible
introduction that assumes no prior knowledge
of Zen Buddhism.
0-609-80466-9 Softcover

Rabbi Joseph Telushkin
THE BOOK OF JEWISH VALUES
A Day-by-Day Guide to Ethical Living
Ancient and modern advice on how to remain honest
in a morally complicated world.
0-609-60330-2 Hardcover

James Thornton
A FIELD GUIDE TO THE SOUL
A Down-to-Earth Handbook of Spiritual Practice
In the tradition of *The Seat of the Soul, The Soul's Code,*
and *Care of the Soul*, a primer readers are calling
"the Bible for the new millennium."
0-609-60368-X Hardcover   0-609-80392-1 Softcover

Joan Tollifson
BARE-BONES MEDITATION
Waking Up from the Story of My Life
An unvarnished, exhilarating account of one woman's
struggle to make sense of her life.
0-517-88792-4 Softcover

Michael Toms and Justine Willis Toms
TRUE WORK
Doing What You Love and Loving What You Do
Wisdom for the workplace from the husband-and-wife team
of NPR's weekly radio program *New Dimensions*.
0-609-80212-7 Softcover

BUDDHA LAUGHING
A Tricycle Book of Cartoons
A marvelous opportunity for self-reflection
for those who tend to take themselves too seriously.
0-609-80409-X Softcover

Ed. Richard Whelan
SELF-RELIANCE
*The Wisdom of Ralph Waldo Emerson
as Inspiration for Daily Living*
A distillation of Emerson's spiritual writings
for contemporary readers.
0-517-58512-X Softcover

*Bell Tower books are for sale at your local bookstore or you may call
Random House at 1-800-793-BOOK to order with a credit card.*

BY THE SAME AUTHOR

SUCH STUFF AS DREAMS ARE MADE ON

The Autobiography and Journals of Helen M. Luke
Introduction by Charles H. Taylor

Helen M. Luke devoted her life to the exploration of the self—both her own and that of countless others who came to her for counseling. She was endowed with a deep grasp of archetypal forces and the ability to evoke them with luminous prose.

Such Stuff as Dreams Are Made On consists of a memoir which she wrote at the age of seventy but never published, and excerpts culled from the fifty-four volumes of journals written in her final years. She weaves together dreams and symbolic images from her inner life with personal and world events, bringing a clear, unsentimental honesty and vibrant insight to all that she recounts. Reflecting on her past as a way of illuminating the present, Luke inspires us to be aware, attend to our personal truths, and "know and accept and live the next thing with devotion." This is Helen Luke's final and magnum opus—her gift to the world.

SUCH STUFF AS
DREAMS ARE MADE ON
Paperback; 288 pages;
$14.95 (Canada: $22.95);
0-609-80589-4
A Bell Tower Book